MW00562737

BRAZILIAN JIU-JITSU MASTER TECHNIQUES

The Essential Guard

Kid Peligro and Rodrigo Medeiros

INVISIBLE CITIES PRESS • MONTPELIER, VERMONT

Invisible Cities Press
50 State Street
Montpelier, VT 05602
www.invisiblecitiespress.com

Copyright © 2005 by Kid Peligro and Rodrigo Medeiros

All rights reserved. This book, or any part thereof, may not be reproduced in any form without permission from the publisher.

Cataloging-in-Publication Data available from the Library of Congress

Anyone practicing the techniques in this book does so at his or her own risk. The authors and the publisher assume no responsibility for the use or misuse of information contained in this book or for any injuries that may occur as a result of practicing the techniques contained herein. The illustrations and text are for informational purposes only. It is imperative to practice these holds and techniques under the strict supervision of a qualified instructor. Additionally, one should consult a physician before embarking on any demanding physical activity.

Printed in the United States of America

Book design by Peter Holm, Sterling Hill Productions
Edited by Tia McCarthy and Carmine Grimaldi, Invisible Cities Press

Kid Peligro

This book is dedicated to all my friends and family and all the practitioners of Gracie Jiu-Jitsu throughout the World, and especially to my wife Susanne, who is my best friend and biggest supporter. To my parents Alice and Gerardo for their unconditional love and support. To my instructors and friends Rickson, Royler and Royce Gracie.

To my best friends Fernando Andreis and Marcus Osorio for the years of friendship

To my friends Carlos and Felipe Gama for hooking me up with Jiu-Jitsu and the incredible sport that it is. To my first Jiu-Jitsu instructor and friend Nelson Monteiro for showing me the first steps in this great art.

To Rodrigo Medeiros for his friendship and the valuable help with this project.

And last but not least to my friends Kai and Robert Garcia for always being there with a good advice and support and for never forgetting what friendship is all about.

Rodrigo Medeiros

I dedicate this book to the two people who supported and encouraged me throughout my life, my parents Armando and Annette Medeiros, and to my master Carlson Gracie. I want to give special thanks to John Sundt from Sundt Memorial Foundation for the years of friendship and the support of the sport of Jiu-Jitsu. To Kevin Fialco, from Lek Shelters, for all the advice, friendship and for always being by my side whenever I need him.

To Richard Colavin, from Veterano Sports, for his inspiration, friendship and his dedication to the academy and all my students.

To all my students in the USA, Brazil and around the World

And to Kid Peligro, my brother and friend, for the immense opportunity to do this work.

Contents

OPEN GUARD TECHNIQUES / 187

Traditional Open Guard / 188

Spider Guard / 198

Butterfly Guard / 214

figure 1: closed guard

Introduction

Gracie Jiu-Jitsu (also known as Brazilian Jiu-Jitsu) has quickly become one of the most important martial arts on the planet. Although developed in Brazil over 75 years ago, the world first took notice in 1993. It was at the first Ultimate Fighting Championship, an event pitting an eclectic mix of fighters against each other, where Royce Gracie demonstrated the power of Gracie Jiu-Jitsu. His most fascinating, and entirely "unconventional" technique, was the guard—it completely flipped the standards of positional dominance upside down. Before, people had always assumed that the fighter on the bottom was losing, but after seeing Gracie Jiu-Jitsu in action, these assumptions quickly died. Royce proved that you could do more than just fight from the bottom. You can win from the bottom.

On that November night in 1993, Royce's victories sent shock waves throughout the martial arts world. Immediately after, an unprecedented number of people were looking to learn the Gracie techniques. The number of practitioners skyrocketed. But unfortunately, this quick spike in demand caused a shortage of qualified instructors. Because of this, many instructors and students haven't had the time, training or adequate instruction to really delve into the intricacies of each position. This demand has led to the Brazilian Jiu-Jitsu Techniques Series, a long sequence of successful books from members of the Gracie family and Kid Peligro.

Up until this point, the series has concentrated on broad aspects of the art, among them self-defense, ground fighting techniques, no holds barred-style fighting and championship techniques. However, because there are some specific elements of Gracie Jiu-Jitsu that are critically important, the necessity of more specialized books became apparent—like *The Essential Guard*.

What is the guard?

The guard exploits the bottom position. Generally speaking, the guard is defined by having your back on the ground and your legs between you and your opponent. There are two major guard positions. If your legs are locked around your opponent, it's called the "closed guard" (see figure 1). This is considered the better defensive guard (although you can initiate a variety of attacks from it) and greatly increases your control. If your lock is broken, you can move into the "open guard" (see figure 2). In this position, without the defensive benefit of a trapped opponent, you must use your feet, legs and arms as a barrier.

Keeping this barrier is essential. If your opponent breaks it, a move called "passing the guard", you can fall into an extremely vulnerable position.

figure 2: open guard

figure 3

figure 4: tripod sweep

figure 5: arm-drag

Passing the guard is described in the International Brazilian Jiu-Jitsu Federation rules Section 4 under points:

B. Passing the guard: The athlete who is above his adversary and between his legs, moves to his opponent's side and thereby establishes a perpendicular or longitudinal position over his adversary's trunk—dominating him and leaving him no space to move or to escape the position, **3 points.** Three points are awarded regardless of whether the athlete underneath is on his side, back, or facing down (see figure 3).

Note: If the athlete underneath avoids the move by getting to his knees or standing up, the initiative will not be awarded 3 points but will be awarded an advantage.

In competition, passing the guard earns three points. But beyond giving him points, passing the guard can give your opponent a stable position to strike and easily control you. For this reason, practitioners of Brazilian Jiu-Jitsu have dedicated a lot of time to studying and creating techniques to maintain and defend the guard.

The guard, however, is not only a defensive position. Over the years, many techniques have been developed and refined to reverse positions or to finish a fight by submitting your opponent. The sweep and the reversal are two effective ways to move your opponent from top to bottom position.

The International Brazilian Jiu-Jitsu Federation describes the sweep in its rules, in Section 4 under points:

F. The sweep: The athlete underneath has his opponent in his guard (between his legs) or in the half-guard (having one of his adversary's legs between his) and is able to get on top of his adversary by inverting his position, **2 points.**

Sweeps occur when the bottom player uses his legs to gain top position. One example is the tripod sweep (see figure 4). Reversals, on the other hand, are generally any other bottom to top switch without use of the legs, like the arm-drag (see figure 5).

Submissions are another set of tools that are critical to developing a strong guard. A "submission" is any type of finishing hold that forces your opponent to submit – conveyed by tapping the body or mat, verbally submitting, or losing consciousness – and end the fight. Submissions are described in the International Brazilian Jiu-Jitsu Federation rules Section 1 as:

1. Submission
Submission occurs when a technique forces an opponent into admitting defeat by:
A. Tapping with the palm against his opponent or the floor in a visible manner,
B. Tapping with his feet on the ground (if he is unable to use his hands),
C. Requesting verbally to the referee that the fight be stopped (if he can neither tap with his hands or his feet), or
D. Requesting that the fight be ended if the athlete gets injured or feels physically incapable or unprepared.

Submissions are generally divided into two major groups, "joint locks" and "chokes". Joint locks usually involve a technique that hyperextends the opponent's joint (see figure 6). The choke, on the other hand, is a grip that constricts the blood flow to the brain, causing a loss of consciousness (see figure 7).

figure 6: joint lock

Why a book about the guard?

The guard is absolutely crucial. In fact, it might be the most important position in Gracie Jiu-Jitsu. During a fight, you spend nearly fifty percent of your time either defending the position or defeating it. There are hundreds of techniques, including sweeps, reversals and submissions, that originate from the guard.

But the guard is not as simple as one plus two equals three. The guard may be one of the most difficult positions to master, full of nuance and small details like hip position and grip that can make the difference between victory and defeat.

figure 7: choke

This book will present drills to improve your techniques and mental reflexes. It will teach you physical details, like hip movement and leg positioning, and mental tips: what to think and plan in each situation. The guard is vast, and trying to explain and understand everything can be a pretty daunting task. So daunting in fact, that no other book has ever tried to fully describe it. In this book, we will concentrate on the essence of the guard to give you a solid framework on which you can build.

Jiu-Jitsu is probably the only martial art that puts such a strong emphasis on fighting from the bottom. While judo has many of the same techniques as Jiu-Jitsu (and many players have excellent bottom game), its object is always to control from the top position. This is also true with wrestling and Russian SAMBO. Even through these disciplines utilize techniques to fight and attack from the bottom, they always emphasize fighting from the top. That's what makes Jiu-Jitsu so strong—it explores and exploits both top and bottom. With the guard, a Jiu-Jitsu fighter can skillfully control his opponent wherever he finds himself. Armed with the guard, and the techniques drilled over and over, a Jiu-Jitsu fighter can confidently and consistently win from the bottom.

Why learn to fight from the bottom?

When you can fight with your back on the ground, you're entering the Jiu-Jitsu fighter's domain. Of course, this doesn't mean you should only learn guard. Far from it. But if you can perfect fighting from the bottom, you will be able to fight bigger and fitter opponents. While they waste energy pressing down and maintaining their position, you can rest, using the ground as your ally. You don't need to exert one muscle to maintain your position when the ground is your backstop.

When fighting from the bottom, your opponent's weight advantage is partially diminished. By using the ground for support, you can transfer your opponent's weight through you and into the ground. Of course, size difference will still exist – between two similarly skilled opponents, the bigger person will still have the advantage – but compared to a standing fight, the advantage enjoyed by the larger fighter will be greatly reduced.

Use the ground as your ally; use it to rest. When you're on the bottom, you don't have to waste extra energy to maintain a position. You can recuperate while your opponent struggles to progress and pass your guard.

Why learn the basics of the guard?

Many people wonder why they should read a book on guard basics. Since the basics are introduced early in training, many people want to learn new things and move on to more complex techniques. These advanced techniques work great at first. You put a couple techniques together and created "your" signature move, catching your opponents with their defenses down every time. But as your opponents get used to your sequence and your game, its effectiveness dwindles. Your game starts to become disconnected and nothing seems to work anymore. Even your signature move has become ineffective. Everything was so fluid and cohesive and you can't figure out what happened.

At times you remember old positions, positions that you once executed so well. They were your bread and butter, but now you barely think of them. This is because your opponent has adapted. If you train with the same people, they probably know your new attacks and have learned to skillfully counter them. This forces you to find new moves, leaving the old ones behind. You are constantly forced to add and change, building in complexity until your technique becomes confused and disjointed

So how do you escape this destructive cycle? The key is in the basics. Now that your new and expanded game is filled with complex and advanced moves, you can inject the basics back into it. In fighting and training you will find you can use the basics ninety percent of the time, while the more advanced techniques will usually work only in rare and specialized cases. Mastering the basics, which you will use so much more frequently than the specialty techniques, will greatly increase your success and your chances of winning. You can use the basics as your foundation, building advanced variations off them, smoothing out and solidifying your game. That's why this book is so important. Not only will it improve your guard, but it will also give you a solid base to adapt and add new and advanced techniques.

The basics are the roots of the tree. If the tree has strong and deep roots, the tree will grow up big and strong. But if the tree roots are shallow, the taller the tree grows, the more precarious its position. The guard is the roots of your bottom game. It's the basis of surviving when you're fighting against bigger and stronger opponents. It's the basis of surviving when you're tired or sick.

Imagine you're challenged to a fight when you're physically exhausted—if you are dependent on fighting from the top, or on having enough stamina, what are you going to do? Tell the challenger, "I'm sorry, I'm feeling a bit under the weather. Can we do this some other day?" By having a good guard, you will have the ability and confidence to take a fight even though you are tired, sick, old, or weak. If you don't fight on the streets – and most people don't – you'll still need it for competition. A good guard will prepare you against an opponent with more stamina, or help you win consecutive fights—like Royce Grace, who's the only person in no-holds-barred history to win four fights against bigger and stronger opponents in one night. If you have a strong guard, you can last forever; you simply fight with your back on the ground as your opponent wastes his energy on the top.

Guard Essentials

For the guard, as in all aspects of Brazilian Jiu-Jitsu, the basics are paramount. Everything develops and builds from them. Just as a strong tree needs solid roots, a strong Jiu-Jitsu fighter needs a solid foundation in the basic techniques. But what are the basics of the guard?

The basics are:
1) Understanding when a position is lost and when to change to the next one
2) Knowing who has control
3) Being able to escape the hip
4) Learning the fundamental techniques such as the cross choke, the arm-lock, and the basic sweeps

The fundamental techniques (and some more advanced ones) are presented later in this book, but let's examine the next three basics first.

figure 8

Understanding when a position is lost

If you recognize the moment when your position is lost, you can to switch to a more advantageous position before your opponent can control you. For example, if you have your opponent in a closed guard and he begins to break it, you need to realize your position is lost and switch to open guard. If you don't, he could gain control of your legs and easily pass your guard. A lot of people erroneously think that keeping the guard closed at all cost is the best strategy—it isn't. If you keep your guard closed to the last second, breaking it only when he forces it open, then you're too late. If this happens, not only will your opponent have broken your closed guard, but he'll have ample posture and balance to be in the right position to grab your pants and control your legs (see figure 8). It would be much better to realize that the position is lost, open your legs sooner, and be able to place your feet in a better position – like one foot on your opponent's hip and the other on his biceps (see figure 9).

figure 9

Understanding what control is and who has it

Control is an extremely important aspect of the guard. As a general rule, remember: *Whoever controls the grip has the advantage in any position.* The person controlling the grips will most likely determine the next step and the next set of actions. If you're in the closed guard and you allow your opponent to control your sleeves, then you're in his control—he can fend off any of your attacks or sweeps, and can posture himself and start to break your guard open. Similarly, in the open guard, if your opponent grabs your gi pants at the ankle, effectively controlling your legs, he has a tremendous advantage and is in a great position to pass your guard (see figure 10). So being able to fight for the grip control – and keeping it! – is absolutely central to guard defense.

figure 10

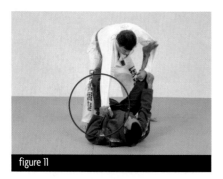

figure 11

figure 12

figure 13

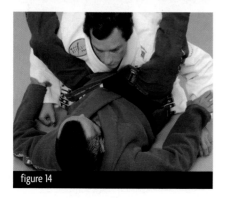

figure 14

The grip is also important to positional control. A fighter with the grip advantage can control the takedown, the guard, the pass and any other position in Jiu-Jitsu. The fight for the grip is a battle that is fought all the time and is won, or lost, by knowledge, anticipation and quick thinking. For example, when two fighters have control of each other's arms, *the fighter who has his elbow bent and closest to his body has control of the grip.* In figure 11, Kid and Stefano control each other's sleeves; Kid using his left hand, Stefano using his right. Notice that Kid's elbow is bent and close to his side while Stefano's arm is fully extended. This gives Kid the flexibility to stretch his arm while Stefano's arm is already completely straight and cannot flex or adjust. Until Stefano is able to bend his arm and bring his elbow closer to his torso, Kid has control of the grip.

In a situation where your opponent has broken your closed guard, he controls your legs, and presses them down as he continues his pass. At this point, there will be another battle for positional and grip control. To regain the advantage, you need to sit up and move your hips back. This will take away some of his controlling advantage (see figure 12). Here is another very important tip for your guard: *Every time the opponent presses your legs down, you need to sit up!*

There is a very important sequence of things you need to remember to have a good guard. It's not so important to be able to win every situation, holding on with all your strength until the last moment. Instead, you should be able to realize what is happening, identify who has control, and understand when your position is lost. This way, you can have time to relinquish your failing position and move to another option or counter ahead of your opponent. Again, in the situation we are examining, the simple sequence would be; "If your opponent opens your guard, you cannot allow him to control your legs. If he controls both your legs, you cannot keep your back on the ground, you need to sit up and move your hips back."

It's easy to see the importance of grip control when looking at the traditional guard pass. If you allow your opponent to lock his hands around your leg and on your lapel (see figure 13), his job is almost complete. However, if you can block his wrist from reaching around your waist (see figure 14), you can maintain control and force him to find another option.

It is extremely important to know when the grips are lost and when to move to the next step. It is absolutely crucial that *you always know the right time to change from one position to another.*

Understanding hip movement

Hip movement might be the most important element in having a top-notch guard. Your hip placement is crucial in both defending your guard and using it as a launching pad for attacks. Where you place your hip in relation to your opponent's torso and hips can drastically impact not only your defense, but it can also effect your sweeps, submissions, and replacing your guard. For these reasons, having a more active hip is an absolute must for improving and developing your guard.

Your hips are the link between the upper and lower body—they transmit power and connect movement. By bending your body at the hips, you can reintroduce a barrier and protect your body from your opponent's control (see figures 15 & 16). Or, if you straighten your body, you can push your opponent away and put more distance between him and you (see figure 17).

figure 15

Your hip can also help control your opponent's weight. Using the hips correctly, you can deflect his weight from where he wants it to where you want it. By moving your hips to one side, you can divert your opponent's pressure, or even take him off balance and force him to choose between retreating, abandoning his progress and grips, or being reversed. Just look at a situation in which your opponent is passing your guard to one side (see figures 15, 16 & 18). If you remain static with your hips, he can pass your right and gain side control. However, if you make a slight technical adjustment – moving your hips in and then back to the center – you can foil the pressure of his pass (see figure 16) and block his path (see figure 18).

figure 16

No matter what guard you're in, your hips should rarely be still. Whether the guard is closed or open, the hips must be constantly active. This is perhaps the hardest thing to teach and one of the most important things to know. With each hip movement you open up new opportunities and possibilities. While there aren't any unbreakable rules in Jiu-Jitsu, this is close to it: *always keep your hips active and out of the center*. The cross-choke (see figure 19) is an exception in being pretty much the only attack from the guard with centered hips. Generally, you should avoid having your back flat on the ground and your hips square in front of your opponent. Whenever you move your hips in and out or from one side to another, you open up new options for yourself.

figure 17

In a static environment, it's relatively easy to teach someone a technique such as an arm-lock from the guard. The mechanics are pretty basic and most students, after a few repetitions, should get the hang of it. But moving the hip properly, in the right direction for an attack or defense, is a different story. It is something that can take years to teach a student—especially to the point where he is fully aware of what he wants to do and where he needs to be.

There are several drills presented in this book that are specifically designed to develop and enhance your hip movement. If you practice them frequently, your guard will improve tremendously.

figure 18

The Three Keys

No matter what guard you are in – open, closed or half – you need to know these three keys:

1) You must be able to replace your guard and keep your opponent from passing it.
2) You should try to submit your opponent.
3) You should try to sweep your opponent and reverse your position from top to bottom.

These three keys are fundamental to your guard. If you want to have an effective game, you will need each one of them.

figure 19: cross-choke

So let's examine them:

1) **Defending and replacing your guard**

It's obvious that if you want an effective guard, you need to defend it well. First and foremost, you must prevent your opponent from reaching side control. You can protect your guard by using your legs as a barrier and moving you hips from side to side and away from your opponent. Preventing someone from passing your guard *includes replacing the guard, turning to all fours or standing up*. In this book, you will find a lot of drills and techniques to help you defend your guard. If used correctly, they'll help you develop a solid game.

2) **Submission attempts from the guard**

While protecting the guard is your main prerogative, you can't only focus on defense. You also need to be on the offense—always threatening your opponent with the danger of submission. If you don't, he can take bigger risks and concentrate on positional gain. On the other hand, if he's faced with the danger of submission, he'll be more distracted, more cautious and give up some of his gains. By partially playing the offense, you add distraction and detract from his overall game.

3) **Sweeps and reversals**

When you attempt a submission, you worry your opponent and detract from his game. The same is true with sweeps and reversals. Bombarding your opponent with them will greatly increase the chaos and decrease his concentration. By adding the element of a possible sweep, your opponent will not only give up positional gains, but will also open up to a possible submission (similarly, submission attempts can open your opponent up to a possible sweep). In Jiu-Jitsu, you always need an arsenal of options. If you have only a few options, your opponent will have an easy time controlling you. So expand your arsenal. The more options you have, the more trouble you can cause your opponent.

As with any attack or aggressive move in Gracie Jiu-Jitsu, submissions and reversals can be a double-edged sword. If you execute such a move unsuccessfully, you can be left in a worse situation than where you started. If this happens, returning to key one will help. Replacing the guard can get you back to a safe and neutral starting point where you can reassess the situation and decide your next course of action.

How do the keys work?

Let's look at these keys applied to a defensive guard situation.

Key #1: Defending and replacing your guard

You have your opponent in the closed guard. You start out attacking his balance and posture; you pull his elbows out and head down, attack his neck and attempt several sweeps. But your opponent is crafty. He counters all of your attacks and maintains his position. After a few exchanges, he manages to gain posture and open your guard. Instead of stubbornly keeping your guard closed, you realize your position is lost and uncross your legs. By quickly realizing your lost position, you can keep the initiative and place your legs on the opponent's hips and biceps. Your opponent continues in his battle for your side, and you counter with some of your defensive skills – recoiling your legs, breaking his grips – but he's still gaining on you. Then he starts to reach for your side. The smart player that you are, you quickly place your hand on his biceps and block his top arm from reaching around your neck.

Every time he attempts to reach your side, you counter with a guard replacement technique. He begins to get frustrated. Every time you throw a block or replacement at him, he becomes more and more aggravated and begins attacking with less control and less concentration. He becomes determined to pass your guard; getting more careless and taking bigger risks. When this happens, you can exploit it, taking advantage of his recklessness and regaining your closed guard.

Key #2: Submission attempts from the guard

You're back in the guard, but you can't defend it forever. Your opponent is bigger, stronger and he has moved into a good stable position. Little by little he's gaining ground in passing your guard; his grip is adjusting and his hands are moving closer to your head. Because his position is so solid, it's not easy to replace the guard and, if you stay in the same situation, he'll have side control in no time. Now let's say you attempt a choke; placing your hand in his collar and distracting him from passing your guard. This might force him to relinquish his grip and move his body back, giving you space to readjust your position and even replace your guard or maybe succeed in securing the submission and ending the match. Playing a simple counter attack, instead of always playing defense, can quickly turn the tide in your favor.

Key #3: Sweeps and reversals

Let's say that your attempted submission forced your opponent to retreat and opened up precious space. With it, you slide your hips out and place your hooks under his thighs, immediately using them and forcing your opponent off balance (see figure 20). Now, he has a few difficult choices to make. If he continues to fight for his current grip and guard pass, your choke will submit him. If he gives up his grip and defends the choke, his hands will be tied up and you could sweep him. Let's say he chooses the former. He decides that a sweep attempt is imminent and tries to defend against it by putting one hand on the mat and bracing himself. With his defense hand preemptively blocking a sweep, you can cinch your hands deeper into his neck. Feeling the immense pressure on his neck, he abandons his brace and moves to defend the choke. His weakness is revealed and you can exploit it. If you lift your hooked leg from under his leg, you can sweep him and end on top!

You can see the advantage of having a big arsenal of options. By using all the guard elements together you can create a situation in which your

figure 20

opponent falls into a lose-lose situation. In the first part of the scenario, he was forced to choose between being choked and letting you replace your guard. In the next part, when you introduced the sweep, he had to either let you replace your guard, be submitted or be swept. This is exactly how your mind needs to work in the guard. You should always be thinking of variations—whichever way your opponent moves, you always have the upper hand.

Developing your understanding and ability to use the keys

You're probably thinking, "That seems simple enough; I'll develop three or four guard replacement options, a few submission attacks, a couple of sweeps and voila, no one will ever pass my guard again!" Well, not so fast. First of all, learning a few combinations and putting together an effective game of attacks, sweeps and replacements takes quite some time. Also remember, while it might seem that your opponent has the disadvantage of choosing between many options in a restricted amount of time, so do you. It might seem simple and easy. But it isn't. When you have to choose between many options – and decide by yourself, on the spot – there is a greater chance of making a bad decision and losing the match. So how do you develop the coordination, the level of understanding and those quick decision-making reflexes necessary for your combination? First, you need to learn the basic positions and master them individually. Second, you need to decide which positions are best for your game, which you most often use, and which have the best results. After that, select two keys; either a guard replacement with a submission, a replacement with a sweep or a sweep with a submission. Drill this two key combo until it's completely automatic. The moment a position occurs that calls for the use of a guard combo, like an imminent pass, you should automatically switch into the one-two combo that you have drilled, going back and forth between the two keys.

Let's say you've chosen a guard replacement with a choke submission combination. In this case, you would attempt the submission, and depending on your opponent's reaction, you would either submit him or replace your guard. If either submitting him or replacing the guard doesn't work the first time, and it rarely does, go back and forth between the two options—try to submit, opponent defends, try to replace the guard, opponent defends, try to advance your choke a little more, opponent defends. Go back and forth until you either replace your guard or submit your opponent. You should do this drill with an easier, lighter partner. Working with a lighter partner allows you to control the direction and pace of the training—determining which techniques are used, deciding to allow him to gain and advance in the pass so you can "power" out of positions, and limiting the training to the techniques and situations that you want to practice. With a less challenging partner, your mistakes will be less damaging, and you can recover, adjust, and repeat the drill more easily. Such repetition will invariably help you learn. Practicing in Jiu-Jitsu is a lot more realistic and intense than in most martial arts. If you try to learn and use the drills with a bigger, stronger opponent, your rate of success will be much lower and you may end up with nothing learned and a passed guard. You will find yourself getting frustrated and less inclined to keep working and may end up discarding the failed techniques altogether. Wait until you have mastered skills before you try going up the size-skill ladder.

Once you've mastered the simplest combination, add another key. To your replacement and choke, you could now add a hook sweep. Repeat the same steps as above. First, master the transition between all three keys, practicing the back and forth movement until it becomes automatic. Again, this is harder than it may seem. Drill and repeat until you have not only trained your body, but have also trained your mind to deal with the extra variable. After you master this, make it a little more challenging by giving your partner more liberty to react. Again: practice, drill and repeat. Then as you become even more comfortable, try adding another variable, like an arm-lock. It should be something that you can do well and works with your previous choices. Practice, drill and repeat.

As you progress, keep adding new elements. Try to add evenly though; don't add a bunch of replacements on top of each other. Always make sure that you have a similar number of techniques from all three keys—in other words, don't have one replacement, one sweep and four submission attempts. After a while though, once you've connected eight or nine elements, you can start to develop one particular key more than the others. But realistically, if you have two good sweeps, two solid submissions and two effective replacements all working in unison, your guard will be awesome! Give it a try!

How do you improve your guard?

If you improve your guard pass, your guard defense will also benefit. But improvement only comes with practice. After learning and practicing the principles presented in this book you will quickly develop a stronger guard. A great way to improve your understanding of what you need to have a great guard is to use the mirror principle: reversing the situation by using what your opponent needs to defeat your guard. Practice passing the guard to learn what it takes to succeed and what sort of difficulties you might encounter when trying to pass an opponent's guard. You'll discover the tools you need: what grips work, where your body weight and positioning should be. Then, when the situation is reversed and you are defending your guard, you'll understand what's important to block, and how to avoid giving your opponent openings. At the same time, you can learn how a good guard defense can effectively stop your pass and know the most effective tools a defender could use against you. Take note of these tools, and incorporate them into your game.

If you're an agile person, you'll execute a position differently than if you're slow or inflexible. Learn the position and adjust it to your physical capabilities. But how do you do that? By practicing, drilling and repeating the position over and over again. As you work and rework it, your body will naturally begin to adjust to it. If you are inflexible and the position requires you to bend backwards, your body will start to find little devices such as spaces or angles to make the position work. So it's important not to give up on a position too easily, particularly if it's one of the basics. If you practice them enough, regardless of your body type, the positions will eventually work.

Jiu-Jitsu is full of personal preferences; some people love the open guard, while others will only fight in the closed guard. Generally, tall people with long legs prefer the closed guard. With long legs, it's really difficult to get enough leverage to open the guard. It's also the ideal position for heavy legs, allowing you to exert more force on your opponent. Little guys with short legs will generally choose the open guard. In this position, the legs can move quicker and he needs less space to bring his legs back in and replace the guard. The same goes for light and fast people. The open guard is perfect for swift legs and quick hips that can move in and out.

By moving your hips to different positions, you can find new angles that not only reveal new options, but also improve your ability to execute them. A smart opponent passing your guard wants to control your hips, even more than your legs. The hips are vital to your defense; if he can control them, he has greatly reduced your options (see figure 21). By controlling the hips, your opponent also limits your ability to use your legs defensively against him.

While drilling, make sure you practice with several partners. Begin with the partner you feel most comfortable with and ask him to let you easily execute your moves. As you progress, get him to increase the resistance or difficulty. Once you have reached the level where you can easily execute the move against him, get a partner who tends to be more challenging. If you find yourself stuck in the same situation every time, go back and review the move with your old partner. Ask him, or an instructor, for advice. Keep working on it until it's really solid.

The Closed Guard

In the closed guard, breaking your opponent's posture is a high priority. If he manages to gain posture — getting his elbows closed, head up and back straight (see figure 22) — then your positional advantage is lost and your guard will probably be opened. So remember: *In closed guard, you need to continuously break your opponent's posture.*

Keeping your opponent close is another priority. If you allow distance between you and your opponent, you diminish the possibility of an effective attack and allow him to gain posture, which is an important element in passing your guard.

figure 21

figure 22

Breaking the opponent's posture

There are several ways to break your opponent's posture:

1) Pulling your opponent's elbows out and forward

2) Placing one foot on the hip while pulling on the sleeves

3) Using your legs to push, pull and move your opponent from side to side

4) Pulling down on the opponent's head

While the technique section contains an in depth analysis on breaking the posture, let's quickly go over some of the common ways:

1) **Pulling your opponent's elbows out and forward (see figure 23)**

    To maintain his posture, your opponent keeps his forward arm straight; forming a block that keeps his torso erect while pushing your torso down and away. If you pull up on his elbows while bringing your legs up towards your head, you can break his barrier. It will cause him to fall forward and into a position without balance or posture.

figure 23

2) **Placing one foot on the hip while pulling down on the sleeve (see figure 24)**

    As previously stated, your hips connect the upper and lower body, transmit power and link movement. It also acts as your center of balance. If you place one foot on the hip, you can effectively control your opponent's balance. By exerting various pressures with your leg, you can bend him, pull him closer or push him further away. Place both hands on his sleeves or sleeve and the other on his collars. If you forget this and simply place your foot on his hip, he can just stand up and move away. This is a great position because it not only keeps your opponent from gaining posture. It's also a nice launching pad for sweeps and attacks like the arm-lock, "omoplata" and choke.

figure 24

3) Using your legs to push, pull and move your opponent from side to side (see figure 25)

When it comes to breaking the posture, people often forget the legs. If you're in closed guard and have your opponent between your legs, you can use your legs to control him. By moving your legs up, down, or from side-to-side, you can effectively move his torso in those directions and keep him from gaining proper posture. But remember—the legs can't do it alone. Simply moving your legs around will only work for a certain amount of time. If you only concentrate on moving your legs, your opponent will eventually ground himself and gain an advantageous position. That's why you shouldn't focus solely on leg control—to break his posture, you need to move your legs in conjunction with other tools.

figure 25

figure 26

4) Pulling down on the opponent's head (see figure 26)

There's an old saying: "Where the head goes, the body will follow!" In Jiu-Jitsu, this couldn't be more accurate. In order to have proper posture, you need to have your back straight, head up and your eyes looking forward (see figure 27). If you pull your opponent's head down, his body will follow, and his posture will crumble.

These, as well as other posture-breaking techniques, will be further explored in the techniques section of this book.

Keeping your opponent close

figure 27

In the closed guard, *it is absolutely crucial to remain close, tight and in contact with your opponent.* If your opponent can distance himself and gain posture, your closed guard has lost its advantage and is in jeopardy of being passed. One good example is the cross choke. If your opponent can keep his distance, you won't have enough leverage to apply the choking pressure, or in more extreme cases, you won't be able to reach his collar. Lacking this control, your opponent could easily gain posture and break open your guard. But if you can bring his head closer, you can reduce your vulnerability and put him in an effective choke. Almost all closed guard attacks work this way. The tighter you are to your opponent, the greater your control.

Another high priority is minimizing distance. You need to stay close to the opponent so you can effectively control and attack him. If he can create distance, your job will be a lot harder. Your opponent's elbow, if uncontrolled, can be very dangerous. If you give his elbow enough freedom to close, you are helping him gain posture. Keep control of his elbows—by pulling them open and out, you can keep him off balance (see figure 28).

When attacking or submitting at the joints, make sure you're aware of hip placement. If you don't press your hips tightly against his joints, your opponent could escape. A good example is the arm-lock from the guard. Your hips need to be up and close to the elbow (see figure 29)—if they are on the ground, too low or away from the joint, your lock will be too loose and he could easily avoid it (see figure 30). You can really damage his defense by constantly attacking his neck with a choke. It will force him to protect his neck, opening him up to a gamut of other dangerous options, like arm-locks and sweeps.

It is also important to always be one step ahead of your opponent. You always need to be thinking about his next move. That way, if you know what his options are, you can have your counters already planned and ready. It's a good idea to plan a strategy based on your best moves; if you are mediocre at an attack, don't use it. For example, you initiate your attack series from the closed guard with a choke. Your opponent defends by posturing and leaning back. In response, you attack his arm with a regular arm-lock, and he defends. Now, you have two options for an attack: the triangle or the omoplata. If you're better at the triangle than the omoplata you should execute the triangle. Since your chances of success are always best with your best weapons, you should always use the moves you have already perfected instead of those you're still learning. This doesn't mean you should limit yourself and not learn new moves, far from it. Rather, when you are fighting, your rate of success will be higher when you use your best moves. Also, your best moves will force your opponent to defend with extra vigor, possibly causing him to over-commit and open up for a new attack. If you use your worst moves or the ones you haven't yet mastered your success rate will be much lower and you may get frustrated and give up on the newer techniques thinking that they don't work or you can't do them or may get so frustrated that you may not even want to train anymore! Since decision making is a great part of the game and a great reason for success, newer techniques should be incorporated in your game slowly and one or two at the time at the most otherwise you will "break your well oiled machine"

When choosing your sequence of moves, the closed guard is a very advantageous position. Because your opponent is between your legs, you have more time to select your next attack. After practicing for a while, you will begin to develop sequences of moves that work well together. This is the essence of Jiu-Jitsu. The more options you have planned and connected, the better chance you have of succeeding. It's like a chess game—to defeat an expert player, you need to have your moves planned turns in advance and adjust to his changes and reactions. This is particularly true at the higher levels. As your opponents' skill levels increase, they will learn how to counter your direct attacks. So you need to constantly change and vary your moves. This will help you get ahead of your opponent, and

figure 28

figure 29

figure 30

eventually, you will execute an attack before he can successfully defend it. This can be tricky; an attack takes longer to perform than its defensive counter, so you need greater precision and quicker anticipation than your opponent.

Since the offense always takes longer to develop than the defense it is very important to not only properly execute the right technique at the right time but actually be ahead of the opponent slightly. Take the arm-lock from the guard, for example, which takes much longer to execute than to defend against. To straighten your body and extend his elbow, you need to control his elbow, then turn and lift your hips, then loop your legs around his head. This takes a while. On the other hand, your opponent simply has to pull his elbow out and your entire attack is dead. To beat him, you need to act quickly and efficiently.

To develop these games and sequences, you should first build off your basic moves. Drill two moves together. Once you've mastered this combination, incorporate a new one and drill again. Keep practicing, perfecting and adding. If you can keep solid form while adding new techniques, your game will be superb.

The closed guard is a great place to work on these sequences. It gives you a lot more time than the open guard, where things move more quickly and developing your game is much harder. Generally, it's pretty easy to execute a single move. The real skill, and this is what really distinguishes purple from black belt, is knowing, selecting and properly applying the perfect move in each situation. Today, purple belts know as much as black belts, but under pressure they don't have the quick mental reflexes. It all comes down to timing—quickly choosing the best move and executing it with precision.

Closed guard attacking stances and grips

There are many ways to establish a controlling grip. Your hand position and controlling grips can vary from controlling both sleeves, to controlling one sleeve with its variations – such as placing both hands on one sleeve with one controlling the wrist and one controlling the elbow (elbow grip), one hand on the collar and one on the sleeve, or a variety of other combinations (like the straight and crossed grips). There isn't a best option—you should choose the grips that work best for you. Of course, this doesn't mean that some grips aren't better suited for certain situations. You should experiment with each grip, develop them and try to master at least a couple. If you increase your arsenal of grip options, you'll become less predictable and more effective.

Controlling both sleeves grip

By controlling both sleeves you take away your opponent's ability to use his arms for posturing. This is a good grip for arm attacks and some sweeps, but it is not effective for chokes. Grab each of your opponent's sleeves, preferably at the wrists, with each of your hands. Keep your elbows tight against the side of your body for greater control. You may grab over the wrists (see figure 31) or grip the gi

figure 31

sleeve cuff with the fingers and curling it (see figure 32). You can use the straight grip, which is more common, by grabbing the arm on the same side with your hand, or the crossed grip by grabbing across the wrists with each arm (you end up grabbing the right hand with your right hand and the left on with the left hand). The cross grip may be harder to achieve as the opponent will quickly sense or feel his predicament but it gives you greater options with arm attacks like the "omoplata", the regular arm-lock from the guard and taking the back while the straight grip is more appropriate for the regular arm-lock from the guard and to transition to the wrist and elbow grip.

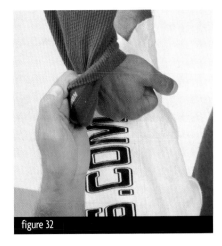

figure 32

The two sleeves grip sometimes is a difficult grip to maintain as you have each of your hands controlling each of the opponent's wrists, making it somewhat of an "equal" power situation, (of course if you are stronger than your opponent you may prevail more often or vice-versa) and you can make it stronger by using the gi sleeve grip described above. This grip is a good grip for the arm-locks and perhaps the best for omoplata attacks and a few sweeps, but again, it is not as effective for chokes.

Wrist and elbow grip

A great way to begin an attack from the closed guard is to establish a controlling grip on your opponent's elbow. With one hand, grab your opponent's wrist and, with the other hand, grab under his elbow on the same side. Place your foot on his hip (the same side as his gripped arm), apply pressure and escape your hip towards the same side (see figure 33). From this position, many attacks will become available. This grip is best for the arm-lock, omoplata, triangle attacks and some sweeps, but not as effective for collar chokes.

figure 33

Once you achieve this position, it's important to correctly time your attack. For instance, if you're in the closed guard with this controlling grip, you should wait for your opponent to make the first move. As soon as he reacts and tries to adjust to your controlling grip, you should immediately execute an attack. This style works for both the closed and open guard. In the closed guard, however, unlike the open guard, there isn't any rush. You can simply wait for him to move, find a vulnerability and attack.

This position has its advantages and disadvantages. One benefit is that you can easily initiate arm-lock, along with sweep, triangle and omoplata combinations. With your foot on the opponent's hip, you can control the distance between you and him and, with your foot pressing the middle of his body, break his posture. Also, in this position, your hips have more mobility, giving you more control and speed. But to get into this position, you need to break your traditional closed guard lock losing some of the control it affords in order to have a more aggressive posture. Keep in mind however that you can still easily go back to the traditional closed guard at any time by simply releasing the foot on the hip, extending your leg past your opponent's body and re-locking the foot.

figure 34: straight hold

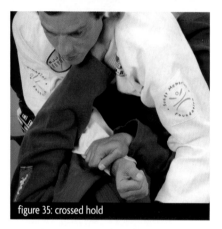
figure 35: crossed hold

figure 36: arm lock

figure 37: scissor sweep

figure 38: standard open guard

Collar and sleeve grip

This is another great position for closed guard attacks. There are two variations of this method; gripping the sleeve and the lapel on the same side, known as the "straight hold" (see figure 34), and gripping the sleeve and the lapel on opposite sides, known as the "crossed hold" (see figure 35).

Both variations have their advantages. Since you dominate his blocking arm until you attack with the submission, the straight hold is best for the cross choke. The same is true for arm-locks (see figure 36). It's also an ideal position if you want to sweep to his controlled side – like the scissor sweep (see figure 37). Since you dominate his collar and arm on the same side, he'll have no way to use his arm to brace against your attack.

The cross hold is best for taking the back with an arm drag or the arm-lock from the guard; the arm drag is a natural choice since you are already holding his forward arm with your opposite arm in perfect position to pull and cross his arm in front of his body, exposing his back. Also, a small hip escape towards his controlled arm will put you in the perfect position for an arm-lock.

While there are many variations of grips, the foundation of the closed guard remains the same: *move your body, using your hips, legs and arms, to break your opponent's posture, then attack with a submission and sweep*. If you want a top-notch closed guard, this sequence should be your mantra.

The Open Guard

The closed guard is a formidable position, but you can't expect to keep it forever. Eventually a skilled opponent will manage to crack open your guard. As we have discussed, you need to know when your closed guard is lost and quickly transition to your favorite open guard control. Swiftly reposition your arms and legs to where they best serve your game. If you keep your legs locked and wait till the last possible moment, your opponent will probably be ahead of you and block your ideal position. Even worse, he could easily pass your guard. So remember: *know when your position is lost and place your controlling grip before your opponent can establish his grip*.

Just like the closed guard, the open guard is far from static; everything is constantly moving and changing. While the speed of change in the closed guard can be slower, with you controlling the pace, in the open guard your opponent's movement is not as restricted. His torso is free from being locked between your legs, so things can and do happen quickly, creating more opportunities for gain and for mistakes to occur not only on your opponent's part but also on yours. Having the techniques and variations mechanically and mentally engraved in your mind so you can quickly and properly decide which option is the correct one will yield even bigger results in the open guard than in the closed one and also will keep you from giving up too much ground with a bad decision on your part. In the open guard, your first line of defense – the closed guard – has already been passed, and your opponent is probing for side control. There are several main open guard positions: the most common and practical are the "standard" open guard (see figure 38), the "spider" guard (see figure 39), the "butterfly" guard (see figure 40). There are also some more complex variations like the "De La Riva" guard (see figure 41), the "X" guard and the "Sit-up" guard. Regardless of which open guard you use, there are certain necessary keys that apply equally to them all.

figure 39: spider guard

There are several important principles to develop to have a good open guard:

1) Use your legs as pistons
2) Action-reaction principle
3) Be aware of your opponent's weight distribution
4) Don't let your opponent control your legs
5) Don't let your opponent control your torso and one leg
6) Don't let your opponent control your hips
7) Maintain your distance while still staying connected
8) Keep your knees open

figure 40: butterfly guard

Use your legs as pistons

Alternately coiling and extending your leg or legs will help you control and maintain distance with your opponent. Acting defensively, you may need to bring your leg, and even your knee, up to your chest (see figure 42) in order to replace a blockade in front of your opponent to prevent him from passing your guard. Once that is achieved you now need to reestablish the distance between yourself and your opponent. By pushing your legs out either to move him away (if he's smaller than you), or push yourself away from him (if he's bigger than you) you can recreate a comfortable distance to re-start your open-guard defense (see figure 43). Other times, you may need to pull him close in order for you to use your attacks. Remember that it's much harder, if not impossible, to submit or sweep someone who is far away from you.

figure 41: De La Riva guard

Action-reaction principle

Newton's third law of motion states that for every action, there is an equal and opposite reaction. When grappling, people are no exception. They will often counter a force with an equal force in the opposite direction. If you push, you'll be met with a push. And if you pull, you'll feel a reactive pull in the opposite direction. When fighting from the guard, you need to be aware of this reaction and exploit it. If you want your opponent to move forward, push him back and he'll naturally react to it by leaning forward.

You should always keep this concept in your mind, particularly when in the open guard. It may seem futile to fight head-on against a bigger, stronger opponent, but this concept will make it possible. A basic principle of Jiu-Jitsu is that avoiding direct power confrontation, along with mastering your opponent's reactions, can give you the power to win. The "action-reaction" concept is central to the open guard. It's nearly impossible to push your opponent away once he has secured the proper grips and is reaching for your side. However, if you redirect his

figure 42

figure 43

pressure and use your arms and legs to push away you can take advantage of his reaction of pushing back by coiling and redirect your push in the direction you want him to go. You can escape his controlling position and even make him vulnerable to a sweep or submission.

While trying to pass your guard, your opponent has secured a grip on your collar and gained the advantage. Rather than fight to break his grip, straighten your body and push him back. In reaction to this, he will counter your push by putting his weight forward. Use this forward push against him by rolling backwards and regaining the defensive position (see figure 44).

figure 44

figure 45

Although it seems very simple, amazingly enough this principle is one of the hardest things to master and actually use in real training and fighting. Most people just try to muscle their way into the technique that they want to use and ignore what the opponent is doing. In this situation, the match becomes a battle of power and strength. Use the action-reaction principle to control your opponent's power, and you will turn his strength into your advantage.

Be aware of your opponent's balance and weight distribution

When fighting in Jiu-Jitsu and especially when using the action-reaction principle, make sure you're always aware of your opponent's body position and balance. By noticing your opponent's weight distribution, you will have a better feel for which moves will work in each situation, particularly for sweeps and reversals. For instance, if your opponent has his weight back (see figure 45), you should use a move that exploits this position. In this situation, it would be much better to use something like a cross-over sweep, which would take advantage of his current lean, than force his weight in the opposite direction with a move like the overhead sweep. It is much more effective to move with your opponent's weight rather than against it. Furthermore, by constantly watching your opponent's balance and position, you can feel a weakness and quickly exploit it with a reversal or sweep. In order to be successful in Jiu-Jitsu, you need vigilance and smart decision making skills; don't force a move in an inappropriate situation.

Don't let your opponent control your legs

This might be the most important key to the open guard. Defensively, your legs act as a barrier, protecting your side and preventing your opponent from passing your guard. Offensively, you need your legs for attacks, sweeps and other moves. If your opponent can control your legs, he can probably pass your guard (see figure 46) and he certainly will diminish your ability to sweep and submit him.

If you lose control of your legs, your ability to move and maintain an ideal distance will also greatly diminish. As we mentioned earlier, pushing with your feet is the easiest way to move your hips and reposition your body. If your opponent can seize control of both of your legs (see figure 47), this tool will be made useless. Even worse, if he can pin your legs down to the mat (see figure 48), he can effectively pin your legs and hips, reducing your mobility. After compromising your ease of movement and eliminating the barrier of your legs, he could easily reach your side and pass your guard.

figure 46

figure 47

figure 48

If you fall into this fragile position you need to get out of it quickly. You can either break his control of your legs (see figure 49), or regain control by circling your foot around his arm, in this case, with one foot over the arm, regaining control (see figure 50). Notice that when he grabs your legs from above he can easily drive them to the ground but when you circle them around his arm with the heel on top of forearm he cannot control them anymore.

figure 49

figure 50

Don't let your opponent control your torso and leg

You can't let your opponent capture half of your top and half of your bottom; such as controlling one arm and one leg (especially on the same side), or one leg and the collar (see figure 51). If you allow your opponent this control, it has a similar effect to controlling both legs; he can either pin you down, easily reaching your side and passing your guard, or he can spin you like a wheel and gain side control.

By understanding what situations and controls you need to avoid, you should be able to see them coming and know how to block them. If that fails, you can quickly break one of the grips, or make another adjustment, and regain the advantage (see figure 52).

Don't let your opponent control your hips

As we explained in "Understanding Hip Movement", hip movement is central to guard defense and offense, and losing it can be catastrophic. You not only lose your ability to attack with sweeps and submissions, but you also give him an easy pass at your guard. Your hips connect movement and power between the upper and lower body—if you give up control of your hips, you ultimately give up control of your body. If you don't quickly break this control, your guard is in big trouble.

By being sensitive to this type of control and knowing the elements necessary to attain it, you can recognize this danger and avoid it. Again, it is much easier to recognize your opponent's motives and preemptively block, than it is to escape (see figure 53).

figure 51

figure 52: pushing the elbow up breaks control

figure 53

Maintain your distance without being disconnected

To pass your guard, your opponent needs to get close. So when you're in the open guard, you need to keep a good distance between you and your opponent. By keeping him at a distance – either by using your legs to push him away (see figure 54), or by moving your hips back and away every time he gets close (see figure 55) – you are blocking him in two important ways. First, you're too far away for him to pass your guard. Second, your distance stops him from pressing down with his weight and trying to control you. If you allow him to do either of these, he's getting closer to passing your guard. Furthermore, by keeping your distance, you can replace your legs as a barrier and keep him from reaching your side.

The seesaw motion (see figure 56), pushing and pulling your opponent, is another effective way to keep your distance. As he tries to deal with this offsetting motion, he will be forced to forget about positional gains and concentrate on readjusting his base and position. With his focus on offense broken, you can move your hips away and escape his control.

A person controlling your legs from a standing position can use his feet and legs to move around to your side, but in the fight for control he is only using his arms while you are able to use both your arms and legs against him. This gives you an immediate advantage and you need to keep it—use your legs to push him away and your arms to control his arms and legs. Because you have this advantage, always keep the possibility of an attack, like a submission (see figure 57) or sweep, in the back of your mind. By adding the offensive element into the fight, you add a new level of chaos that can throw off your opponent. If he focuses solely on passing your guard, his moves will be more aggressive. However, if you initiate some attacks, he'll have to keep his balance and defend his neck and limbs from submissions. It will make his task much harder.

Staying connected with your opponent

While you need to maintain distance, this doesn't mean you should be completely out of touch. In order to have an effective open guard, you need to remain connected with your opponent. Simply put, your feet and/or hands need to remain touching your opponent at all times. If they aren't, you won't be able to control his limbs, feel his weight placement, or gauge his actions and reactions.

Most sweeps involve using your arms, legs, hands and feet to dislodge your opponent's weight in certain directions. If you aren't constantly connected with your opponent, making necessary adjustments will be impossible, and your submission attempts will fail. Additionally, many submissions require your hips to be near the opponent's joints and, if you aren't connected, these joint locks and submissions will flounder. By maintaining contact, you will not only know your opponent's intentions, but also have an easier time executing submissions and sweeps.

Keep your knees open and not to one side

When positioning your knees, there are two things you need to remember. First, your knees should always be pointing out. Second, they should never be on one side of the body. By keeping your knees pointing out (see figure 58), you are keeping a solid barrier on both sides of your body. You're also presenting a broader barrier, and therefore one more difficult to bypass. If you bring your knees together you are removing this barrier. Similarly, if you put your knees solely on one side, you are giving your opponent a clear path to your other side. Imagine your knees, feet and hips as forming a diamond; knees pointing out and feet pointing in (although not necessarily touching each other). While your opponent would like to bring your knees together and pin them to one side, this position will make his task much more difficult. It will also give you greater ease in executing escapes, sweeps and submissions.

figure 54

figure 55

figure 56

figure 57

figure 58

The Half-Guard

figure 59

The half-guard is a transitional position for the defender—it is his last chance to prevent the opponent to pass and for the passer it is his last hurdle before achieving side control. In guard defense, the half-guard is the last line of defense before having your guard passed, therefore your mistakes may result in having your guard passed or worse being submitted. While in modern Brazilian Jiu-Jitsu there are a great variety of sweeps and attacks from the half-guard, it is not the object of this book to try to cover them as you can write an entire volume on the half-guard alone.

Typically in the half-guard you trap one of your opponent's legs between your legs, impeding his movement to your side for the complete pass (see figure 59).

Using exercises to improve your guard

Improving your game is not easy. Generally, there are two ways to improve your technique: drilling and sparring. Traditional drills or static repetition are a good way to work on the mechanics, but you need a partner who is willing to spend a lot of time practicing with you. Sparring also has its drawbacks. Because your sparring partner will have his own style and preferences, it could be difficult to successfully execute and repeat a technique. Also, when sparring, you are less likely to try new moves, worried that you might fail and get stuck in a bad position. To really improve your game, you need to do both. You should drill and repeat your techniques with a willing partner, then apply them in a sparring session.

In this book, you'll find a lot of recommended drills and exercises to improve your guard. They will force you to repeat and focus on one specific aspect of the game, helping you learn the nuances and intricacies of each position. Unlike sparring, when you practice drills, the outcome is predetermined: you can repeat it over and over and learn from your mistakes. Here are a couple examples:

A Defend the guard with one arm stuck inside your belt
B Defend the guard with two arms inside the belt
C Defend the guard with the main objective of sweeping your opponent
D Defend the guard with the main objective of submitting your opponent

These drills not only focus on using your legs and escaping your hips, but also limit your available weapons. By restricting the use of your arms, for example, you can better learn how your other body parts need to work. It will help balance your guard, emphasizing each individual aspect.

The drills should be done in this manner: Set a certain amount of time and try to defend the guard while your partner attempts to pass it. When the drill is finished – regardless of the winner – try it again. Keep repeating until the drill is perfect.

Meet the Team

Author

Kid Peligro

One of the leading martial arts writers in the world, Kid Peligro has regular columns in *Bodyguard* and *Gracie Magazine*, as well as one of the most widely read Internet MMA news pages, *ADCC News*. In recent years, he has been the author or coauthor of an unprecedented string of bestsellers, including *The Gracie Way, Brazilian Jiu-Jitsu: Theory and Technique, Brazilian Jiu-Jitsu: Self-Defense Techniques, Brazilian Jiu-Jitsu: Black Belt Techniques, Brazilian Jiu-Jitsu: Submission Grappling Techniques,* and *Superfit*. A first degree black belt in Jiu-Jitsu, his broad involvement in the martial arts has led him to travel the four corners of the Earth as an ambassador for the sport that changed his life. He lives in San Diego.

Author

Rodrigo Medeiros

When it came time to select a co-author for this book, Kid didn't hesitate to ask his good friend Rodrigo Medeiros for assistance. Rodrigo is a third degree black belt and member of the powerhouse Carlson Gracie Team. Widely considered one of the best and most technical instructors in Brazilian Jiu-Jitsu, Rodrigo is an active competitor and holds many prestigious titles, including a World Masters Title and several Pan-American Titles.

Rodrigo is the leader of the BJJ Revolution Team and his school, Pacific Beach Fight Center, is in San Diego, where he also resides.

Assistant

Stefano Aguiar

Stefano Aguiar has been Rodrigo Medeiros's leading assistant instructor for many years. An extremely skilled brown belt with a high level of technical expertise, Stefano oversees the youth programs at the Pacific Beach Fight Center and is one of the academy's leaders. He lives in San Diego.

ESSENTIAL GUARD TECHNIQUES

There is nothing more essential in Brazilian Jiu-Jitsu than the guard. Mastering it allows you to fight against bigger opponents and under difficult situations. In the next pages important drills and techniques will be presented to improve and solidify your game. The techniques are designed to give you a solid base to your guard game. Mastering these techniques will give you the tools and knowledge you will need to effectively react to the situations you are most likely to encounter. You will also gain the skills to create and expand the game on your own.

Mastering these techniques and concepts is not going to be easy but with practice and repetition you will reach your goal. The reward will be a guard game that will be effective, efficient and dangerous to your opponents. Now go to it.

Drills

Drills are the best way to replicate and learn moves used in training and competition. Repeating them several times in a row will quickly improve both your understanding and mechanics. Eventually it will imprint itself on your neuro-muscular system and become automatic.

When executing a drill, it's important that you begin slowly and always concentrate on form. Your speed will increase with repetition. If done well and with proper form, your twentieth repetition should be better than your tenth. But make sure you don't just concentrate on speed. If you practice a drill incorrectly, the sloppy move will be imprinted on your neuro-muscular system and it will be a lot harder to fix.

Make sure to practice these drills to both sides in equal number of repetitions so you can be adept at executing the moves on both sides. We recommend practicing each drill at least ten times from each side.

This is one of the most important drills you can practice. While it's usually associated with escaping from the mounted position, it can also be used in other situations. This drill will not only develop your technique, but also improve your hip movement, giving you a "loose" hip. This drill is a perfect way to start any training session.

1 Kid begins by lying down on his back with his legs extended. The heels should be touching each other while the elbows, bent at the side, are touching the mat.

2 Kid coils one leg back while turning his body towards the opposite side. In this case, Kid coils his right leg, keeping his right foot against his buttocks and firmly planted on the mat. He then turns to the left, away from his curled leg.

3 Pushing off with the right foot, Kid pivots on his left shoulder and moves his hips to the right. Jackknifing his body, his torso is almost at a ninety-degree angle to the legs. While doing this, Kid brings in the left leg. Notice that Kid's body is completely turned to his left and how his left elbow takes away any space by touching his left knee. Kid plants his left toes on the mat.

4 Kid pushes off with the toes to re-center his body, ending with elbows and knees coiled together.

5 Front view Kid plants and pushes off with his right foot, while pivoting on his left shoulder. You can repeat this drill from your original starting position or you can continue moving along the mat in a straight line.

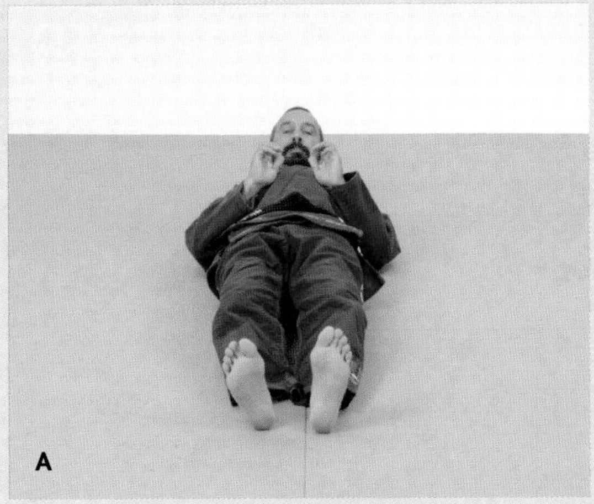

A

B

C

D

A very common and effective way to defend someone from passing your guard is to turn to all fours or, as it is often called, "turtling". Of course, turtling should be the last resort—it's much better to intercept and defuse an attempted guard pass earlier, but sometimes it's the only way to stop your opponent from reaching your side. This movement is used, with minor variations, in several techniques; like the butterfly sweep and escaping from side control.

1 Kid starts by lying on his back, legs extended. He coils the right leg back, planting the right foot as close to the right buttock as possible.

2 Kid pushes off with the right foot and pivots on the left shoulder while raising the hips. He brings the left leg in and under the bridge formed by the right leg and his hips.

3 Still bridging with the right foot and left shoulder, Kid shoots his left leg back, planting the left toes on the mat as he turns his torso to the left.

4 While pushing off with his right foot, Kid turns over and coils the left leg so that his chest parallels, and both knees touch, the ground. Kid then pushes off his elbows and coils his hips back so that his buttocks are nearly touching his heels. Kid ends on all fours with his knees and elbows on the mat.

The square drill is one of the best drills in Jiu-Jitsu—it replicates several fighting moves, develops balance and body control, and loosens up your hips, shoulders and knees. It's also a fun drill. Experiment and develop your own pattern. Try to repeat it several times; you can alternate directions every couple turns or just stop and reverse your direction at any time during the drill. The key is to always move the foot to where the opposite hand is, shooting the leg under the hips and the hand going to where the opposite foot was looping it over the hips.

1 Kid starts with the palms and feet planted on the mat, hips up off the mat. At this point, his weight is equally distributed between the four supporting limbs. Kid checks his balance before starting the drill; he rocks his body back and forth and side to side, feeling the weight change between each of the four points.

2 Bracing with the right foot and left hand, Kid raises his hips and brings his right hand and left foot off the ground. Kid swings the left foot under the hips and reaches forward with the right hand.

3 Kid brings his left leg back as his right hand loops forward. The goal is to place the left foot where he had his right hand, and to place his right hand where he had his left foot. Once he has achieved this, Kid pauses and re-checks his balance.

4 Continuing in the same direction, Kid pivots on his right hand and left foot, shooting the hips forward while driving the right leg under his body and placing it where his left hand had been. He loops the left hand back, placing it where his right foot had been. Kid's body has now completed a 180-degree turn and is in the same initial position, but facing the opposite direction.

5 Kid continues with the drill. Now, he combines the right hand and left foot. You can continue in the same direction until you return to the starting point, or you can go back and forth, stopping and reversing positions during any point of the drill. As your technique improves, try increasing the speed.

This drill is great for improving your arm-drag technique. It will also help you work on hip movement and mobility when in a seated position. Because many guard movements occur from the upright seated position, this drill will teach you how to move your body from side to side.

1 Rodrigo sits up with his legs in front of him, bent at the knee, feet planted firmly on the ground. The arms, semi-flexed, are outside of the knees with the hands reaching out.

2 Rodrigo plants his left hand and drops the left leg on the mat. Notice that at this point, Rodrigo uses his left hand and right foot as balance points, which he will later use to raise his hips off the ground. Rodrigo extends his right arm as if he were grabbing an imaginary opponent's right arm.

3 Rodrigo braces with his right foot and left hand and raises the hips off the ground. As he does this, he pushes his hips toward the left hand and shifts his leg position, raising the left leg so that the knee points up and dropping the right leg to the mat. As these movements occur, he simulates pulling the opponent's arm across his body. Notice, while Rodrigo begins with his right foot as a brace, when he moves his hips across, he needs to shift that weight to the left foot. This allows him to put his right leg on the mat and complete the motion.

4 To repeat this movement in the opposite direction, Rodrigo plants his right hand on the ground and reaches with the left hand to grip his imaginary opponent's left arm.

5 **Side view of the movement** Notice that Rodrigo's hips move in a semi-circle as they shift from side to side. The weight transfer from the buttocks to the feet and hands is the key to this movement. By pushing with his planted arm to shift the weight from buttocks to feet, Rodrigo makes his hips light and easy to move from side to side. The drill is in fact harder than the actual move. In a fight, Rodrigo would "drag", or pull, his opponent's arm across his body, making it easier to move to the side. This can also be done as a two-person drill.

Because many guard passes involve stacking your legs over your head, you need to have good flexibility to successfully defend the guard. This drill will help you with one important aspect – touching you toes over your head – along with general hip flexibility. Remember, blocking your opponent's path to your side is crucial in defending the guard. If you can swing your legs 360° around your head, your ability to create these barriers and frustrate your opponents will increase.

1 Rodrigo starts by lying on his back with legs stretched forward and arms at his sides.

2 Rodrigo pushes with his right foot, rolls to his left side and, as he rolls on his left shoulder, slightly coils in the legs.

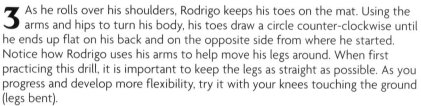

3 As he rolls over his shoulders, Rodrigo keeps his toes on the mat. Using the arms and hips to turn his body, his toes draw a circle counter-clockwise until he ends up flat on his back and on the opposite side from where he started. Notice how Rodrigo uses his arms to help move his legs around. When first practicing this drill, it is important to keep the legs as straight as possible. As you progress and develop more flexibility, try it with your knees touching the ground (legs bent).

4 Rodrigo continues turning in a counter-clockwise direction and rolls over his left shoulder. He continues this circling until he ends up in his original position. Once he completes a full circle, Rodrigo commences the same drill in the opposite direction. Make sure you practice both sides—this will keep your flexibility symmetrical.

Drilling is great because you can repeat your techniques with or without a partner. Repetition is key; it will help you get any move down so you can implement it at the correct moment in a match. The triangle drill is valuable because it allows you to repeat the submission several times in a row and really get the mechanics of the movement. You can practice it on one side for a while and then move to the other, or alternate sides with each repetition.

1 Rodrigo begins on his back, legs flexed at the knees while his arms are at his sides.

2 Pushing off with his hands, Rodrigo lifts the legs up and over his head.

3 With his legs over his head, Rodrigo can lock his legs in the "triangle". He slightly pivots the hips towards the right while bending the left leg down and in. Then, Rodrigo locks the right leg over the left foot at the crease of the knee. He can either reverse the triangle while his hips are still up, or he can return to the starting position and restart the entire move. If you want to change triangle sides without returning to the starting position, you need to rock back and forth, dropping your hips slightly down towards the mat as you reverse sides. Notice that the hips always move towards the leg that locks over the foot.

This drill simulates replacing the guard when your opponent reaches "north-south" position. It will also improve your hip movement and understanding of body positioning, particularly when your legs are over your head – a common situation when defending the guard.

1 Rodrigo lies on his back with the legs extended forward. He is in front of Stefano, who is standing over his head. Rodrigo reaches up with his arms and grabs the back of Stefano's ankles.

2 Pulling himself by the arms, Rodrigo raises his legs over his head and crosses them so that his left is above his right. His right foot touches Stefano's left thigh and his left foot touches the outside of Stefano's right thigh.

3 Rodrigo releases his handgrip and opens his arms wide for balance.

4 Pushing off with his right foot (the bottom leg), Rodrigo pivots his torso around in a clockwise direction, finishing by facing Stefano and bracing his feet against Stefano's thighs. Notice that Rodrigo always turns in the direction of the leg that was on top. Do this drill at least ten times on both sides, alternating every repetition or after a set of ten on one side.

This is similar to the previous drill, differing in that you hook your opponent's legs with only one foot. You swing the other foot, using its momentum to whip your body around and face your opponent. Along with replacing the guard from north-south position, this drill also teaches you how the leg swing moves your body.

1 Rodrigo lies on his back with his legs extended forward. He is in front of Stefano, who is standing over his head. Rodrigo reaches up with his arms and grabs the back of Stefano's ankles.

2 Pulling himself by the arms, Rodrigo raises his legs over his head and crosses them so that his right foot hooks the outside of Stefano's left thigh. His left leg, in contrast to the previous drill, loops over his right leg and remains bent.

3 Rodrigo pushes off his right foot and begins to rotate his body.

A

B

C

4 As his torso begins to rotate, he kicks his left leg out and swings it clockwise. This helps his body spin around. He finishes by facing Stefano and connecting his feet with the top of Stefano's thighs. Like the previous drill, you should repeat this ten times on each side, alternating every repetition or after a set of ten on one side.

This is a fantastic drill—it will teach you to you use only your legs and feet to move your body around the opponent and, in this case, get to his back.

1 Lying on his back and facing Stefano, Rodrigo places his feet on the top of Stefano's thighs. He slips his hands inside his belt so he won't use them during the move.

2 Pushing with his right foot, Rodrigo first swings his left leg out wide, then wraps it around Stefano's right leg, coiling it until his left foot locks on the inside of Stefano's thigh.

3 Rodrigo plants his right foot on the mat and pushes off with it several times, scooting his torso around Stefano's right leg. As he nears Stefano's side, Rodrigo adds to his mobility by changing his left foot hook from the inside of Stefano's right thigh to the front of Stefano's left knee.

4 As he starts to reach Stefano's back, Rodrigo hooks his right foot behind Stefano's right leg. Rodrigo uses this hook to bring himself completely around, ending up behind Stefano and with his feet hooked inside Stefano's legs.

This is a variation of the traditional hip escape drill. Using a partner gives the added benefit of something solid to push against and a real target to replace the guard. Concentrate on your form while doing this drill. As you escape your hip, make sure you keep your head in while pushing your hip out as far as possible.

1 Rodrigo lies on his back with his legs slightly bent at the knees. Kid is standing facing Rodrigo, his right ankle touching Rodrigo's right hip.

2 Rodrigo places his hands on Kid's left knee, using them as a brace. He pushes off with his left leg and turns his body to the right, bending at the waist as he pushes his hips to the left and away from Kid's legs. Notice how high and far to the left Rodrigo's hips move. Also, note how Rodrigo brings his head close to Kid's legs. These details help Rodrigo escape his hips while keeping the rest of his body close to Kid.

3 When he reaches his full escape range with his knees past Kid's legs, Rodrigo brings his outside leg in (in this case the left leg since he is turning to the right) and hooks the foot on the inside of Kid's right leg.

4 Rodrigo pushes with this hook, sliding his right leg under the left and in front of Kid as he brings in his hips. Notice that Rodrigo moves his head away from Kid, giving more space for the move and simulating the set up for a possible sweep. As Rodrigo completes the move and replaces the guard, he ends up with both feet inside Kid's legs and his hips centered in relation to Kid.

This is a variation of the previous drill. Instead of escaping the hips out and away from your opponent's legs, this drill will show you how to escape the hips in front of his legs. This move can be used in many instances. It's particularly useful if your opponent has turned you to one side and is passing towards your back and you can't turn your hips 180° and escape to the outside. Then your best option is to escape your hips in front of your opponent's body.

1 Rodrigo lies on his back with his legs slightly bent at the knees. Kid is standing to his right, his ankle touching Rodrigo's hip.

2 Bracing as if against an imaginary object to his left and pushing with his right (or inside) leg, Rodrigo turns his body left, escaping his hips to the right and toward the centerline of Kid's legs. Again, notice how Rodrigo bends at the waist, driving his head down and towards Kid's leg.

3 Rodrigo then brings in his left (or lower) leg, hooking his foot inside and near the ankle of Kid's right leg.

3 Detail Notice how Rodrigo hooks his left foot inside Kid's right leg.

4 Pushing off with his left leg, Rodrigo circles his right leg to the center. The spin is complete when he can hook his right foot inside Kid's left ankle and his hips are square in front of Kid.

The stacking method is a common way to pass the guard. This is when an opponent under-hooks one of your legs, stacking them over your head and passing under. This drill simulates a counter to that, working your hips and legs at the same time.

1 Kid is lying on his back and his legs are open. Rodrigo places his right hand on the mat in front of Kid's left leg, blocking it while using his left arm to underhook Kid's right leg, placing the hand on Kid's chest.

2 Rodrigo begins to move to his left – the direction of the pass – as he drives his left arm up and forward, turning to the left and lifting Kid's right leg. At this point, Kid plants the toes of his left foot on the mat.

3 Kid pushes off his toes and escapes his hips left. He bends his right leg, brings it towards his chest circling the foot around Rodrigo's head and slides his knee under Rodrigo's left armpit, blocking Rodrigo's path.

4 As soon as his right knee is in place, Kid loops his left leg over and around Rodrigo's head, resting it on Rodrigo's left shoulder and further blocking the pass. Notice that Kid's right foot hooks Rodrigo's right hip. In a real sparring match, this would prevent Rodrigo from quickly changing direction and passing Kid's unprotected side.

5 Rodrigo reverses the direction of his pass attempt, placing his right arm under Kid's left leg and passing to his right. Kid repeats the drill to that side: he plants the right foot, escapes the hips to the right, brings the left knee under Rodrigo's right armpit and loops his right leg around his head. Continue the drill alternating between sides.

This drill simulates taking the opponent's back from the butterfly guard, or simply creating more space for a sweep. It's great for developing total body coordination and strengthening both the legs and core. Notice that, if done correctly, you and your partner will continuously move away from the starting point.

1 Rodrigo lies on his back with his legs bent and his feet hooked inside Kid's legs. This is the butterfly guard position. Kid has his knees and elbows close together, effectively keeping Rodrigo's legs bent and the heels close to his buttocks. Rodrigo grips Kid's gi at the shoulders.

2 Rodrigo uses his grip on the gi to pull Kid's shoulders up and towards his head. At the same time, he kicks up his legs and curls his knees in the same direction, giving him extra power to move Kid's body forward. Notice that the motion is up and over, not up and away. At full extension, Kid feels very light and is under Rodrigo's complete control.

A

B

C

3 As Rodrigo reaches his full extension and has Kid in the air, he begins to push with his arms and legs, driving Kid back and away from his head. While pushing, Rodrigo uses the rocking motion, raising himself and following Kid. Once Kid lands away from Rodrigo on the mat, Rodrigo sits up and drives his head into Kid's chest, wrapping his arms under Kid's armpits and pulling himself in slightly closer while still maintaining proper distance between his and Kid's hips.

This drill simulates an arm-lock from the guard. Rodrigo uses his foot on Kid's hip to escape his hips and create the proper set-up for an arm-lock. Since the arm-lock from the closed guard is one of the position's premier attack weapons, being able to quickly and properly execute it is paramount to having a good guard so drill it often.

1 Kid is inside Rodrigo's closed guard with his hands on Rodrigo's chest. Rodrigo grabs Kid's wrists, his thumbs pointing towards his head.

2 Rodrigo opens both his legs while curling up the left leg. This makes room to place the sole of his left foot on Kid's right hip.

3 Pushing off with his left leg, Rodrigo escapes his hips to the left and places his right leg under Kid's left armpit. Notice that Rodrigo's leg is bent at the knee and his calf presses against Kid's left shoulder. As Kid begins to lean to the right, Rodrigo closes his left leg trapping Kid's right shoulder. Also notice, when Rodrigo escaped his hips to the left, his head circles to the right, towards Kid's left knee. In this position, Rodrigo is ready to initiate an arm-lock on Kid's right arm.

4 Rodrigo continues the drill by reversing directions: he curls up his right
leg, puts the sole of his foot on Kid's left hip and places his left leg
under Kid's right armpit, driving it to the right and down while he locks his
right leg trapping Kid's left shoulder.

In the previous drill, Rodrigo placed his foot on Kid's hip to help his hips escape. This time, to escape the side and deliver the arm-lock, he'll use leg movement and its momentum. Both set-ups are equally effective. It's a matter of preference; the first one gives more control, the second one is faster. It's best to practice this drill by alternating sides with each repetition.

1 Kid is inside Rodrigo's closed guard with his hands on Rodrigo's chest. Rodrigo grabs Kid's wrists, his thumbs pointing towards his head.

2 Rodrigo opens his legs wide while bringing them both up and towards his head. This will place most of Rodrigo's weight on his shoulders, freeing his hips to move from side to side.

3 Swinging with his right leg, Rodrigo spins his hips to the left, pulling his left knee in and extending his right leg under Kid's left armpit. By pushing down and to his left with his right leg, Rodrigo knocks Kid off balance, forcing him to the left. As this happens, Rodrigo loops his left leg over Kid's head and arm-locks Kid's right arm.

4 Pushing off with his right leg, Rodrigo opens his left leg up towards his head and then swings it backs around to the right. This generates the necessary momentum to move his hips to the right.

5 Once his left leg is pressed against the area near Kid's right armpit, Rodrigo pushes off it, propelling his right leg around until he can lock it over Kid's head and arm-locks the left arm.

In this drill, Rodrigo once again uses the leg swing to move his hips from side to side.
This drill is good for sharpening both your left and right arm-locks.

1 Kid is inside Rodrigo's closed guard with his hands on Rodrigo's chest. Rodrigo grabs Kid's gi sleeves at the wrist, his thumbs pointing towards his head. Notice, this time, Kid's arms are crossed over to help the arm-lock.

2 Rodrigo opens his legs and swings them up towards his head, transferring his weight to the shoulders.

3 Swinging with his legs, Rodrigo slides his hips to the left as he pulls Kid's left arm. Notice, since Rodrigo is attacking Kid's right arm, he pulls the left arm to assist in the movement, and moves his head towards Kid's left knee. Rodrigo presses down on Kid's back with his right calf, making it easier to swing his left leg over Kid's head and lock the arm.

4 In order to move his body to the other side and attack the left arm, Rodrigo swings his legs up and over, releasing the lock, while pulling Kid's right arm.

In this drill, Rodrigo swings his legs up and over Kid's shoulder, quickly locking his legs and trapping the arm for a lock. In this case, Rodrigo has one hand on Kid's collar and the other gripping the targeted arm.

1 Kid is inside Rodrigo's closed guard with his hands on Rodrigo's chest. Because Rodrigo is planning to trap Kid's right arm, his right hand grips Kid's collar and his left hand holds Kid's right sleeve at the elbow.

2 In one motion, Rodrigo opens his legs and swings them up while escaping his hips to the left.

3 Once Rodrigo has placed his leg over Kid's shoulder, he locks his legs by crossing his feet. Notice that Rodrigo's left thigh is over Kid's right shoulder, trapping it and exposing his arm for an arm-lock.

This drill is based on the arm-lock from the guard. It can be viewed as a technique or, as in this case, can be used to drill the most basic arm-lock from the guard. Repeat this drill at least ten times on each side before switching. This is great a warm up before training.

1 Kid is inside Rodrigo's closed guard with his hands on Rodrigo's chest. Rodrigo traps Kid's right arm—with his right hand he holds Kid's collar, with his left he holds Kid's right elbow at the sleeve.

2 Rodrigo pulls on Kid's right arm as he swings his legs up and pivots his hips to the left.

3 Pushing his right calf down against Kid's left side helps Rodrigo turns his body to the right. He circles his left leg around Kid's head, locking it above Kid's shoulder and trapping the left arm. Notice that Rodrigo doesn't release his left hand, blocking Kid from pulling his arm out. To complete the drill, Rodrigo drives his heels down pressing his calves down on Kid's back.

Techniques: Replacing the Guard

This is one of the keys to having a great guard. As we previously stated, it's almost impossible to always prevent someone from passing your guard, especially if you're attempting a submission or sweep, which are effective moves that can also leave you more vulnerable to your opponent's counter-attack. When attempting attacking moves – or even in standard guard defense – you may make mistakes or your opponent may get into an advantageous position, crack your barrier and pass your guard. To defend against this, it's crucial to be able to quickly and effectively replace the guard.

As you become more confident and capable at replacing the guard, your attack techniques will improve. If you're always worried about losing your guard position, you attacks will be less aggressive and effective. But, when you have confidence in replacing your guard, you can be more assertive—if your opponent passes your guard, you can simply replace it and try again. Additionally, when you have a great guard replacement you will not only frustrate and tire your opponent but you will also keep yourself relaxed, even as your opponent appears to pass your guard, as you know that you will quickly be able to replace it.

The stacking method is one of the classic ways to pass someone's guard and gain side control. In this method, the passer underhooks one or both of the defenders legs. He then chooses a side, grips the opposite collar and lifts the defender's legs, "stacking" them over his head. The ideal course of action would be to block the opponent's grips and position before he could even make the pass (see the introduction, figure 13). In this case, you would try to prevent the opponent from underhooking your leg or, if that failed, prevent him from gripping the opposite collar. But sometimes, the opponent is able to secure a great position, like the one shown below. In this case we pick up the pass with Rodrigo underhooking Kid's right leg and gripping the left collar as he attempts to pass on the right side.

1 Rodrigo underhooks Kid's right leg with his left arm and grips Kid's left lapel with his left hand. He then stacks Kid's legs over his head and passes to the left.

2 Kid must first break Rodrigo's control over his hips. With his right hand, Kid pushes Rodrigo's left elbow up until it clears Kid's right knee, opening up space to coil his right leg and bring the knee under Rodrigo's armpit. Notice that Kid plants his left toes on the mat and pushes of the foot to help arch his body to his left. **Expert Tip:** the key here is using the right arm to push the elbow up, creating space rather than fighting to block the hip with a stiff arm.

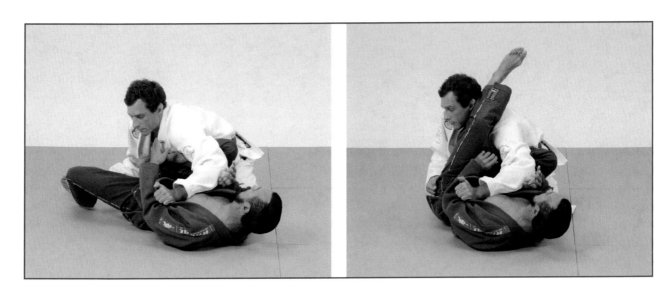

3 Kid then pushes off his left heel, turning his body to the right, and loops his left leg over Rodrigo's head. By resting it on Rodrigo's left shoulder, he effectively blocks a left pass, while his right foot protects the other side.

4 Having successfully blocked Rodrigo's pass, Kid pushes with his left calf and scoots his hips back to the center. He finishes the guard replacement by putting his left leg back on the left side over Rodrigo's right arm.

In this scenario, Rodrigo attempts to pass Kid's guard using the double underhooks variation of the stacking guard pass. This guard pass is not as common as the previous one but, because double underhooks allow the opponent to pass on either side, it's highly effective.

1 Rodrigo underhooks Kid's legs with his arms and locks Kid's hips by clasping his hands together. Rodrigo stretches his body, raises his torso off the mat with his feet and begins to stack Kid's legs over his head. This is the critical point. If Kid doesn't regain his hip control, his guard will likely be passed.

2 Kid drives his hips forward and straightens his body as if he were kicking up. He then places both hands on Rodrigo's elbows, pushing them up as he drops his hips down. This combination allows Kid to bring his knees under Rodrigo's arms and break his control. Rodrigo's grip and control is very strong and tight, so it's absolutely necessary to follow the sequence; first you straighten the body and then drop the hips down as you simultaneously push on the elbows.

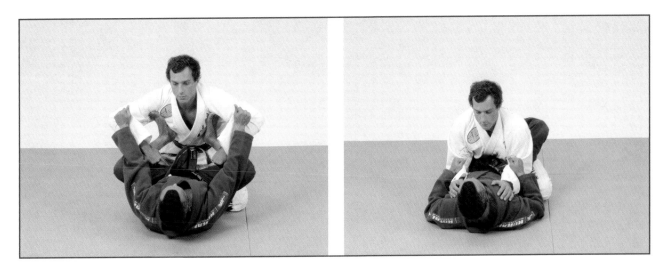

3 Kid continues to push Rodrigo's elbows up as he further coils his legs. This gives him the necessary space to bring his feet in, lock his legs around Rodrigo and solidify the closed guard.

Another way to defend against the double underhook stacking pass is to roll over while your opponent is choosing sides, reaching for the collar grip and trying to stack you. The opponent's forward pressure will assist your shoulder roll.

1 Kid has underhooked Rodrigo's legs with his arms, locking his hips by clasping his hands together.

2 Kid springs up, beginning to stack Rodrigo by throwing his legs up and over his head.

3 Kid reaches his right arm around Rodrigo's left leg until his hand grips Rodrigo's left collar at the neck. Rodrigo immediately blocks Kid's left hand from grabbing the bottom of his pants—this grip would prevent Rodrigo from rolling back. Notice how Rodrigo grabs Kid's left wrist and pushes the arm out. This technique would not work if Kid grabs Rodrigo's pants under the buttock because he would hold the pants down, stopping Rodrigo from rolling over his shoulders.

3 Detail Rodrigo uses his left arm to lock Kid's right hip, both to protect him from getting to his side and to help him propel his legs over.

4 Kid continues to press forward, further stacking Rodrigo's legs and preparing to pass his left side. Rodrigo takes advantage of this pressure; he simply extends his body and lets the pressure push his legs over his head. He then rolls over his right shoulder.

5 His roll ends with his right knee on the ground and his left leg extended out, both legs braced to control the roll. Rodrigo continues the roll as he brings his right knee in and scoots his hips in while using his right arm to traps Kid's left leg. Rodrigo can sit back and replace the guard, or he can explode and take Kid's back by lifting the head and going under Kid's right arm.

In this variation, Rodrigo defends against the double underhook stacking method by breaking Kid's grip and moving into the butterfly guard. It's always good to have multiple options, and you can choose between these methods based on your preference for open or closed guard.

1 Kid has secured his grip around Rodrigo's legs and is beginning the stack. Rodrigo grabs Kid's wrist with his hands, the four fingers on top and the thumb under.

2 In one explosive move, Rodrigo extends his body and thrusts his hips up, breaking Kid's grip. Rodrigo uses his hands to keep Kid from closing the grip again. Notice that Rodrigo didn't break Kid's grip with his hand, but rather with the body thrust.

3 Rodrigo continues to keep his hips straight and legs out, bending his legs down until his feet are firmly on top of Kid's thighs. While using his arms to pull Kid's arms, he pushes off with his feet, moves his hips back, and slightly sits up. Notice that Rodrigo changed his grips from the wrists to the sleeves, improving control.

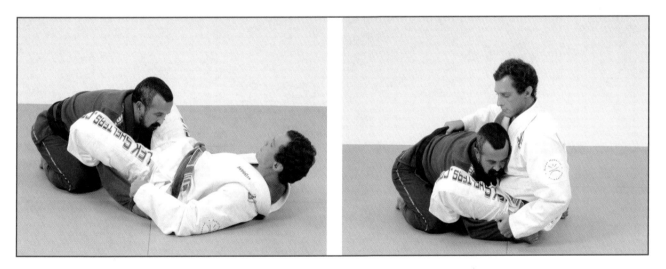

4 Having created distance with the previous move, Rodrigo now hooks his feet inside Kid's thighs. He then releases the grip from Kid's left sleeve and sits up, grabbing Kid's belt with his right hand. At this point, Rodrigo has not only replaced his guard, but is perfectly set up for a hook sweep.

When fighting from the bottom, you'll often find yourself in the half-guard. This is when your opponent has broken your first barrier; either by breaking your closed guard or evading your open guard's leg blockade. Because your first-tier defense, the full guard, has been broken, it's important to have several options for your second-tier defense. By executing a solid defense, you can stop your opponent's progression before he can reach side control, or worse.

1 Kid is in Rodrigo's half-guard. In this case, Rodrigo has trapped Kid's right leg between his legs. His top priorities are proper defensive posture, keeping ideal distance and insuring optimum hip mobility. For this, Rodrigo's left hand braces Kid's left shoulder, the forearm pressing against Kid's throat. This will reduce Kid's forward pressure. Rodrigo presses his right arm against Kid's left side, hindering Kid from moving his hips in and closing the distance. Rodrigo's left foot is planted on the ground while his right leg preserves the half-guard by resting over Kid's right leg. It is extremely important for Rodrigo to remain on his side. If his back is flat on the ground, his hips will be trapped.

1 **Reverse detail** Rodrigo places his left forearm under Kid's chin and presses his throat.

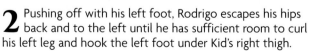

2 Pushing off with his left foot, Rodrigo escapes his hips back and to the left until he has sufficient room to curl his left leg and hook the left foot under Kid's right thigh.

2 **Detail** Rodrigo hooks his left leg under Kid's thigh just above the knee. If Rodrigo hooked below the knee, Kid could simply turn, point his knee inwards and slip his leg out. Also, notice how Rodrigo keeps Kid's right leg trapped until he can hook Kid's left foot. If he didn't, Kid would have his leg free to move forward and reach side control.

3 Rodrigo kicks his left leg up, raising Kid's right leg. If Kid resists, he'll be swept over to his left, which will be even worse for him. By moving his leg with Rodrigo and keeping his hips somewhat parallel to the ground, Kid counters the sweep; he then braces with his left arm and posts open his left leg in order to prevent the sweep attempt. This creates more space for Rodrigo. He quickly brings his right leg in front of Kid's leg, locking his right heel on the outside of Kid's left thigh. At this point, Rodrigo centers his hips, locks his legs around Kid's torso reaching closed guard.

4 **Reverse angle** Notice how Rodrigo first escapes his hips out and back, allowing him to place a hook while remaining on his right side.

Rather than hooking your opponent's leg, sometimes it may be easier to bring your leg in front of his arm. This is the case if your opponent drops his hips, is short, or if your legs are long. Even if you don't encounter these scenarios, you can still use this replacement as another option in the half guard.

1 Rodrigo is holding Kid in the half-guard, trapping his right leg. His right hand braces against Kid's left hip, while his left forearm pushes against Kid's throat.

2 Rodrigo raises his left elbow and presses the forearm harder against Kid's throat, forcing him to retreat. At the same time, Rodrigo curls his left leg, plants the foot on the mat as far back as possible and pushes off with it, escaping his hips back and to his left. Rodrigo keeps Kid at a distance by leaving his forearm on Kid's throat and his right arm on Kid's hip. With the space created by his hips moving back, Rodrigo can curl his left leg and place it in front of Kid's right shoulder.

A

B

C

3 Rodrigo uses his left hand to grab Kid's right sleeve at the wrist, and presses his left shin against Kid's biceps controlling the arm. He then opens his left leg, forcing Kid's body to the left. This allows Rodrigo to bring his right leg in, clearing his knee past Kid's left arm, and return his hips to the center. Rodrigo places his right shin on Kid's left biceps and grabs Kid's left arm with his right hand, gaining control and replacing the guard. Should he choose, Rodrigo can move into the closed guard by wrapping his legs and locking the feet around Kid.

This is another great guard replacement from the half-guard. In this case, Kid, while defending his guard, is able to get his right arm under Rodrigo's left arm. If you can't get into this position, use one of the other options. However the arm got there – maybe in the heat of a scramble, or maybe Kid bumped up and moved the arm in and under the armpit – this is a great option for replacing the guard. Of course, Kid could simply lock his legs tightly and try to preserve his half-guard at all cost, but this would be counterproductive and only result in a stall. Kid would rather replace the guard!

1 Kid has Rodrigo in the half guard, trapping his left leg. Notice, since Kid's right arm is under Rodrigo's left he can use this technique. Kid presses his left leg down on top of Rodrigo's leg to trap it, freeing his own right leg. Kid's left hand is pushing against Rodrigo's right hip to maintain distance

2 With his right leg freed in the previous step, Kid plants his right foot back and to his right, and pushes up, sliding his hips back and to the right. At the same time, he drives his right arm up under Rodrigo's armpit as if he were trying to reach an imaginary object over Rodrigo's right. This forces Rodrigo's torso up and creates space for Kid to curl his right leg in until he can hook the foot under Rodrigo's left thigh. Notice that until he is able to hook the thigh, Kid keeps Rodrigo's left leg trapped by pressing with his left leg, otherwise, with a free leg, Rodrigo could simply pass the guard on Kid's left side.

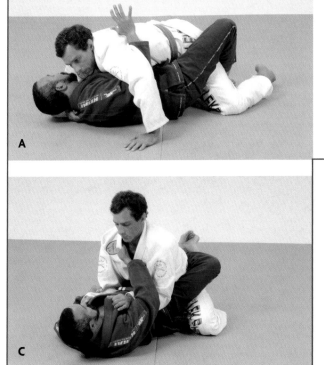

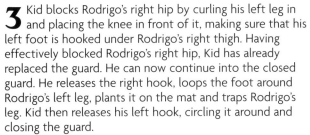

3 Kid blocks Rodrigo's right hip by curling his left leg in and placing the knee in front of it, making sure that his left foot is hooked under Rodrigo's right thigh. Having effectively blocked Rodrigo's right hip, Kid has already replaced the guard. He can now continue into the closed guard. He releases the right hook, loops the foot around Rodrigo's left leg, plants it on the mat and traps Rodrigo's leg. Kid then releases his left hook, circling it around and closing the guard.

3 Reverse view Notice how Kid moves his hips right and then back to the center as he brings his left knee in front of Rodrigo's right hip.

Because of its stability, side control is one of the best positions your opponent can reach. With his chest pressed against you and his hand placement making it difficult for head or hip movement, escaping side control takes significant technical skill. So master the options presented here. In this case, since Kid's lower arm (further from the head) is on the outside next to Rodrigo's body, Rodrigo uses the bump and hook method to replace the guard.

1 Kid has side control over Rodrigo. His right arm is wrapped around Rodrigo's head, keeping Rodrigo from turning left. Kid's knees are in close, preventing Rodrigo from easily bringing his leg in and replacing the guard. Kid's left elbow is tight against Rodrigo's side, further locking his body in place. Rodrigo's right arm is in front of Kid's chest and his left hand holds Kid's pants at the left knee.

2 Rodrigo first needs to create a little space to maneuver. He plants his right hand on Kid's right shoulder and lifts his elbow up, driving his forearm against Kid's throat. Rodrigo pushes off with his right leg and bridges to his left as he continues to press against Kid's throat and, drive Kid's left leg back and off the mat with his left hand. Notice that Rodrigo's left leg flattens on the mat, while remaining bent, as he bridges, or bumps up.

3 Rodrigo takes advantage of the space created by the bump, sliding his left leg under Kid's right knee until he can wrap the foot over Kid's calf. Pushing off with his right foot, Rodrigo slides his hips away and to his right. Notice that Rodrigo continues to force Kid's torso away by driving his forearm into Kid's throat.

4 Rodrigo now slips his right foot under Kid's left leg and hooks it. He then opens his left arm behind him and uses it to prop up his torso. At the same time, Rodrigo pushes off his legs and slides his hips back, re-centering his body and replacing the guard.

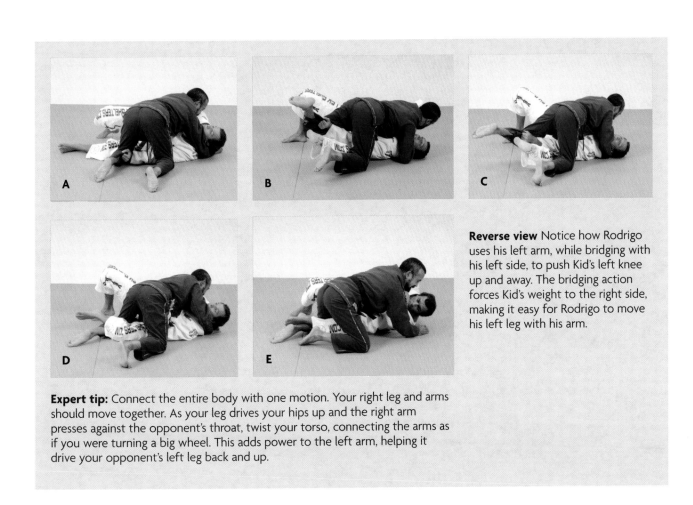

A

B

C

D

E

Reverse view Notice how Rodrigo uses his left arm, while bridging with his left side, to push Kid's left knee up and away. The bridging action forces Kid's weight to the right side, making it easy for Rodrigo to move his left leg with his arm.

Expert tip: Connect the entire body with one motion. Your right leg and arms should move together. As your leg drives your hips up and the right arm presses against the opponent's throat, twist your torso, connecting the arms as if you were turning a big wheel. This adds power to the left arm, helping it drive your opponent's left leg back and up.

In the previous technique, Kid's lower arm was outside Rodrigo's body, allowing him to use the bump and hook method. In this case, however, Stefano's arm is on the inside next to Kid's body, making it difficult to hook with the outer leg. Faced with this limitation, Kid uses the hip escape method. Both methods begin the same way: the forearm pressed against the throat and an upward bridge.

1 Stefano has side control over Kid. His left arm is next to Kid's hip, blocking Kid from coiling his left leg in front of Stefano's hips and replacing the guard. Kid plants his right hand on Stefano's right shoulder, braces his forearm and pushes against the throat, while his left hand grabs Stefano's right sleeve near the elbow.

2 Kid moves his right foot out and back to get a better angle. Pushing off with it, Kid bridges up and to his left, dropping his left leg to the ground and escaping his hips to the right, while driving his forearm against Stefano's throat to create space between their chests. Kid then curls his left leg in while bringing his hips back, forcing his knee between Stefano's left arm and leg until his shin is in front of Stefano's hips.

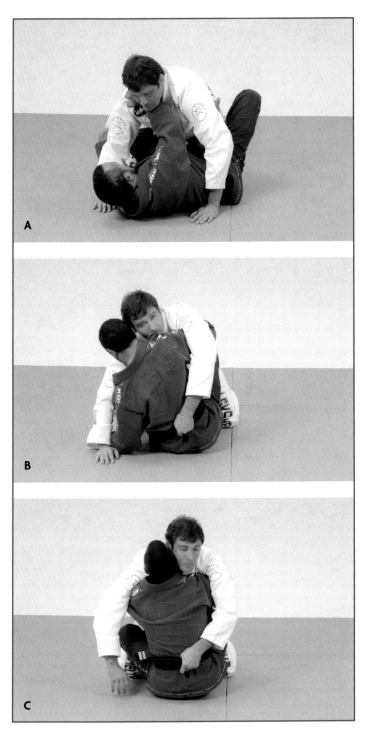

A

B

C

3 Kid braces with his arms, moving his torso away from Stefano while hooking his right foot inside Stefano's left leg. Notice, in order to maintain distance, Kid's right forearm is constantly pressing against Stefano's throat. Kid opens his left arm back and pushes off with his hand, getting his back off the ground and sitting up. He slides his right arm under Stefano's left armpit and grabs Stefano's belt. He then wraps his left arm around Stefano's right side, locking it around his back and replacing the guard.

This is a good alternative to the previous method, particularly if your opponent keeps his elbows and knees tight. If his left knee is forward and tight, both against your hips and his left elbow, it may be difficult to slide in your knee as you escape. Unlike the previous drill, Kid has his right arm *under* Stefano's left armpit. By using it wisely, he can drive Stefano's arm open, creating enough space to bring in his knee.

1 Stefano has side control over Kid. Notice that his left arm is on Kid's left hip, and that his chest and knees are tight against Kid. Kid's right arm is under Stefano's left armpit. He takes a big step out with his right foot and plants it on the mat. He then pushes off with it, slides his hips to the left, drops his left leg to the mat and drives his right arm up as if he were reaching for an object behind Stefano's body.

Expert tip: To have the proper leverage, it is extremely important that you keep your body connected at all times. In this case, Kid has the pressure from his right leg going all the way to his right shoulder driving against Stefano's chest (the body works as one without any give at the waist or any other part, the pressure from the foot pushing up transfers through the "connection" all the way to the shoulder). Don't release pressure simply because you escaped the hip. If you do, your opponent will be able to press your shoulder down, getting your back flat on the mat and regaining side-control.

2 Depending on Stefano's reaction, Kid has two possibilities. If Stefano doesn't press back, Kid can simply continue to step out and move his hips away in a clockwise direction until he can turn onto his stomach and get on all fours. The normal reaction, however, is for Stefano to lean forward and apply pressure, attempting to flatten Kid's body and force his back on the mat. In response to this, Kid pushes harder off his right leg and drives his right arm under Stefano's left armpit, forcing Stefano's weight away from Kid's chest. Stefano pushes back with his chest. Kid immediately takes advantage of this reaction by curling and driving his left leg in front of Stefano's hips. He then brings his right leg in, hooking the foot under and inside Stefano's left thigh. Notice, by driving his right arm up, Kid not only keeps Stefano at a distance, but also moves Stefano's left arm, which is blocking Kid's left knee.

3 With his left knee blocking Stefano's right hip and his right foot hooked under Stefano's thigh, Kid controls the situation. He then moves his head and torso away from Stefano, while moving his hips to the center. Kid pushes off Stefano with his legs, slightly sliding his hips back in order to sit up and get his back off the mat.

When your opponent has a knee pressed on your stomach, you're in a tough position. The pressure drains your stamina and may force you to react too quickly, giving your opponent submission opportunities. The key to escaping the knee on the stomach is to move as soon as your opponent reaches the position and before he solidifies his posture and balance. Also, by keeping your arms near your body, you protect yourself from a potential arm-lock.

1 Kid has his right knee on Rodrigo's stomach. Notice that Kid's grip is not yet finalized, therefore his position is not yet complete. Rodrigo immediately places his hands on Kid's knee, while keeping his legs bent and ready to explode. Notice that Rodrigo doesn't fully extend his arms, keeping his elbows tight against his body. This minimizes space and protects him against a potential arm attack.

2 In one swift motion, Rodrigo pushes with his legs and turns to his right, while escaping his hips to the left. He keeps his arms braced forcing Kid's knee away from his stomach and towards the mat. Notice that Rodrigo doesn't use his arms to push Kid's knee away, but rather uses them to brace and keep the knees in place.

2 Alternate view Notice that Rodrigo drops his right leg to the ground while positioning his left foot so that, if necessary, he can push his hips away.

3 With the space created, Rodrigo loops his top leg (in this case, the left) over Kid's leg and hooks his foot inside of Kid's right thigh.

4 Rodrigo uses his left leg to move his hips back in and slides the right knee in front of Kid's right knee, making sure to keep his right foot hooked on the outside of Kid's thigh.

5 Rodrigo grabs Kid's right elbow with his left hand, releases his right foot hook and, by re-centering his hips in relation to Kid, replaces the guard.

This is a very effective way to combat the knee on your stomach and replace the guard. Using the bump, Rodrigo takes away the pressure by transferring Kid's weight up to his head, making Kid's leg very light and allowing Rodrigo to move and trap it.

1 Kid has his right knee on Rodrigo's stomach. Rodrigo's legs are bent and both his arms are semi-extended, the elbows against his body and the hands braced against Kid's right knee. This time, Rodrigo grabs Kid's pants at the knee.

A

B

C

2 Rodrigo pushes off with his legs, bridging up to his right while gripping Kid's right knee with both hands. As Rodrigo bumps, Kid is thrown forward, forcing him to use his arms to regain balance. With Kid's weight forward his right leg is temporarily lighter, allowing Rodrigo to push it back and trap it by looping his right leg over Kid's at the calf.

3 Rodrigo releases his grip on Kid's knee. He reaches around Kid's back and grabs the belt with his left hand. With his right hand, he braces Kid's right knee. At this point, Rodrigo has escaped the knee on stomach and can close his legs, achieving half-guard.

3 Reverse Notice how Rodrigo's hand placement – the left around Kid's back grabbing the belt, the right one, braced on Kid's left knee – keeps Kid from closing his leg down to the ground. If Kid could get his left leg to the ground next to Rodrigo's hip, it would reduce space and prevent Rodrigo from replacing the guard.

4 While pulling up on Kid's belt with his left arm to keep him leaning forward, Rodrigo loops his left leg and hooks the foot inside Kid's right thigh. Using his legs and hooks, Rodrigo re-centers his hips and replaces the guard.

Whether you're fighting in a tournament, on the streets or in a friendly sparring session, you need to prepare for the worst. Many times, for one reason or another, you'll end up in a bad situation. Don't panic. Make sure you've prepared several solutions. In this case, Rodrigo has mounted Kid. The mount and taking the back are the two highest scoring positions in tournament Jiu-Jitsu, awarding four points. Being able to replace the guard from the mount isn't just important—it's paramount. In this case, Kid uses the "hip escape" method to replace the guard. The tricks to this method are the hip movement out and back, and the arm frame used to block the hips.

1 Rodrigo is mounted on Kid. His knees are touching the ground and his hands are out for balance. Kid's legs are bent and the feet firmly planted on the mat.

2 Pushing off with his left foot, Kid turns his body to the right and drops his right knee to the mat while extending the leg. Kid makes a frame: his arms bent at the elbows, hands pressing against Rodrigo's left hip. Kid's left elbow is bent so his forearm is parallel to Rodrigo's waist and the hand is pressing against Rodrigo's left thigh near the hip. The right elbow is braced against the ground and the right hand is on top of the left hand for support.

2 **Detail** Since Kid is turned to his right, it is very important that the right hand is on top of the left hand for support. This way, the pressure and weight from Rodrigo's body will transfer from the left forearm to the right, which is braced on the ground. If you arrange your hands the other way – your left on top of the right – there's far less support. Notice the frame is used to block Rodrigo's hips, not push them back!

3 Having made his frame to block Rodrigo's hips, Kid pushes off with his legs and escapes his hips up and to the left until they pass Rodrigo's legs and he can place first his left knee, then the right one, in front of Rodrigo's hips. Notice, as Kid executes the hip escape, his head actually moves in the direction of Rodrigo's left knee, helping him bend his body at the waist. It's a common mistake for beginners, and even some experienced fighters, to keep the body straight, not bending at the waist, and try to "push" their hips out from the mount. You shouldn't push your body out; instead, escape the hips back and to the side. It may take one or two hip escape movements, along with the leg coil and push, before Kid's knees can clear Rodrigo's hips.

A

B

C

4 Once his left knee clears Rodrigo's hips, Kid continues to move his hips away to make more space. Kid coils his right leg and opens out his left until it points past Rodrigo's torso and hooks the foot under Rodrigo's right thigh. Notice that at this point, Kid's torso is straight and he is facing Rodrigo as he opens the right knee, hooking the right foot under Rodrigo's left thigh. Kid has effectively escaped the mount and replaced the guard. He immediately sits up, to keep his back off the ground ending up in the butterfly guard.

4 **Detail Expert tip:** Always clear the top knee first, opening it out as a block, before you completely bring in your lower knee. Otherwise, the passer can pancake your legs down and immediately regain the mount.

The elbow escape is another great way to overcome the mount. In this variation, rather than make a frame and escape the hips, Rodrigo will escape one leg and trap Kid's leg, then escaping his other side afterwards. Both methods work equally well – the one you choose is a matter of personal preference. In the previous method, you finished with the butterfly guard; for this method, you'll end with the closed guard.

1 Kid is mounted on Rodrigo. Rodrigo has good posture: his elbows are close to his body and the hands are protecting his collar and neck from chokes.

2 Rodrigo curls his left leg and plants it on the mat, keeping his right leg straight and flat on the ground, turns to his right and places both hands on Kid's left thigh. Rodrigo pushes off with his left leg and raises his hips from the mat in order to lift Kid. Notice, at this point Kid's knees are either off the mat or have very little weight on them, making room for Rodrigo's legs to slide out under them.

3 Rodrigo kicks his right leg out under Kid's left knee, and loops it over Kid's left calf, trapping it. He plants his right foot on the mat. By trapping Kid's left leg, Rodrigo has already achieved the half-guard.

4 Rodrigo repeats this motion on the other side. He turns to his left, places his hands on Kid's right thigh and slides out his left leg under Kid's right knee.

5 Instead of trapping Kid's right leg like he trapped the left, Rodrigo swings his left leg around until his foot comes over Kid's back. He releases his locking right leg and moves it behind Kid's back, locking it and closing the guard.

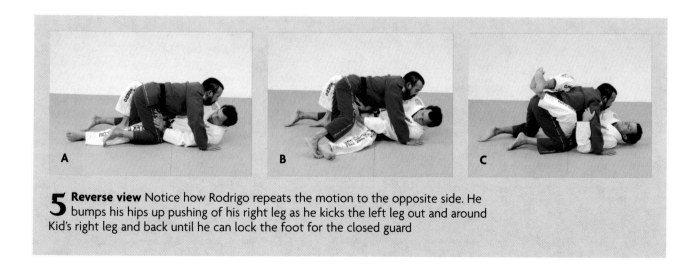

5 **Reverse view** Notice how Rodrigo repeats the motion to the opposite side. He bumps his hips up pushing of his right leg as he kicks the left leg out and around Kid's right leg and back until he can lock the foot for the closed guard

This is another effective way to escape the mounted position. Again, as with the other methods, the point is not to push your opponent's hips away with your arms, which would be extremely difficult, particularly against a heavier opponent. Rather, you need to brace the opponent's hips with your arms and create a way to escape the legs. In this case, Rodrigo lifts Kid by bridging up, or "bumping", using his arms to brace and lock Kid's hips at the highest point. Because you don't need to turn sideways, this method works well as a quick escape when your opponent has just mounted you.

1 Kid is mounted on Rodrigo. Rodrigo has both legs curled and his feet planted on the mat. His hands are on Kid's waist, preferably holding the belt.

2 Pushing off with his legs, Rodrigo bridges up, lifting Kid along with him. At the height of the motion, Rodrigo extends his arms to brace Kid's hips and keep them locked in place. Rodrigo quickly drops his hips, curling in his legs and placing the knees in front of Kid's hips. Notice that the direction of Rodrigo's bridge does not push away, but lifts Kid up and towards Rodrigo's head.

2 **Front view** Notice how Rodrigo bridges as high as possible pushing with his legs. Then, while keeping Kid away with his arms, he quickly curls his legs in till his knees are in front of Kid's hips.

Once his knees are in front of Kid's hips, Rodrigo lets go of the arm brace, dropping Kid down while hooking his feet under Kid's thighs. At the same time, Rodrigo wraps his arms around Kid's back and locks the hands together. Rodrigo then kicks his legs forwards, sits up, and reaches a perfect butterfly guard.

Replacing the Open Guard

As we discussed in the introduction, when you're in the open guard, you can't let your opponent control both of your legs. If he wins control, your guard is extremely vulnerable. In the next few techniques, we'll show several ways to regaining control of your legs in the open guard.

Incorrect Kid allows Stefano to pin his legs on the mat and fails to sit up. Stefano simply puts his weight on his arms pinning Kid's leg down and leans forward, passing the guard.

A quick way to regain control when your opponent grabs both legs over the top is to circle the legs around until until you can lock the heels over his forearms.

1 A classic guard passing technique is to control the legs and pin them to the ground. In this situation, Kid grips Stefano's sleeves at the wrists and his feet are inside, and pushing against, Stefano's arms. Stefano, however, grabs Kid's pants at the knee and wins the battle for grip control. He then straightens his arms, releasing Kid's leg pressure and, if Kid fails to respond, Stefano can push them to the mat.

2 Before Stefano can push Kid's feet down, Kid quickly circles his legs down and around, placing his feet over Stefano's arms. With this move, Kid regains grip control.

You can regain open guard control by circling one leg.

1 Kid has the open guard: his hands gripping Stefano's sleeves, his feet on Stefano's left biceps and right hip. Stefano grips Kid's pants at the knee.

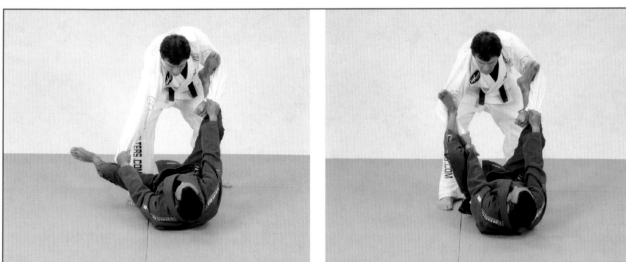

2 Kid still has control over the right leg with his foot pressing against the biceps but Stefano is going to push Kid's left leg down with his right arm, so Kid opens the left leg out and circles it over the arm locking his foot over the arm while pressing the heel down. With one hook over and one under Kid has great control over Stefano's arms.

Breaking the grip is a quick way to regain the guard. In this case, a hard kick out while holding your opponent's gi sleeves will do the trick.

1 Kid has the open guard; his hands gripping Stefano's gi sleeves, his feet on the left biceps and the right arm. Stefano grips Kid's pants at the knee. He then lifts his right elbow releasing the pressure and the control of Kid's heel pushing down on it.

2 Kid shoots his left leg out and straight up into the air, simultaneously pulling down on Stefano's right sleeve with his left hand. This quick kick and pull breaks Stefano's grip on Kid's leg, allowing Kid to recoil his leg and place the left foot against Stefano's right hip. With this, he regains control.

If you're late and let your opponent control and pin your legs to the ground, use this method.

1 Kid has the open guard, but Stefano grips Kid's gi pants, controlling the legs. Stefano pushes the legs to pin them to the mat.

2 Kid quickly reacts to Stefano's control. He sits up because he doesn't want to end up flat on his back.

3 **Side view** Kid plants his left arm back, slides his right arm under Stefano's left armpit and, at the same time, shifts his hips to the right. His left leg is flat on the ground while his right knee is propped up. In this position, Stefano can't pass to Kid's right—Kid's right arm blocks him. Every time Stefano tries to walk past Kid's left, Kid simply pushes off with his left arm and slides, like a semi-circle, to the right. Kid makes sure to keep his hips squarely in front of Stefano

3 **Reverse view** Notice Kid's arm position

4 Incorrect Kid makes sure his arm is inside Stefano's arm under the armpit, otherwise he exposes his arm for an attack

5 Incorrect Kid allows Stefano to pin his legs to the mat and doesn't sit up. Stefano simply puts his weight on the arms pinning Kid's leg down and leans forward passing the guard

The turtle position (turning to all fours) is a common defense against the guard pass. Because your opponent will most likely end up on your back, it's usually used as a last resort. But it's better than having your guard passed and giving your opponent three points in a competition. Since it's so useful, you should know how to move from it and replace your guard. This takes some flexibility and you may not prefer it. If you do master it, however, it can prove extremely effective in replacing the guard.

1 Rodrigo has turned to all fours in the turtle position. Kid is on Rodrigo's back and has gained control by wrapping his arms around Rodrigo's waist. Rodrigo keeps his elbows in and his knees close, taking away the necessary space for Kid to loop his leg around and place a hook.

2 Rodrigo places his left leg (the closest to Kid) between Kid's legs, hooking his foot over Kid's right calf.

3 Reaching his left hand through his own legs, Rodrigo grabs Kid's gi pants on the outside of the right knee. At the same time, he plants his right arm and leg out. He then pushes off them, kicking the right leg over Kid's back and rolling forward over his left shoulder. Kid can't stop the roll. He either lets go of the grip around Rodrigo's back or he will be flipped. Notice that Rodrigo keeps his left foot hooked over Kid's right leg throughout the move.

4 Once his back is on the ground, Rodrigo pushes off Kid's shoulder with his right arm and moves his hips and torso back, creating the necessary space to coil his right leg. He places his knee in front of Kid's torso and hooks his foot on the left side of Kid's ribcage, blocking him from moving to that side. Rodrigo then brings his hips back to center and raises his left knee, leaving his left foot hooked inside Kid's right thigh. He completes the guard replacement by putting his right foot on Kid's left hip and gains control by grabbing Kid's arms with both his hands.

This is another great way to replace the guard from the turtle. If you have less flexibility, or difficulty rolling over your shoulder due to an injury, this will probably be easier to execute. On the other hand, if your opponent is larger and applies a lot of pressure, this may be a little more difficult to perform. In that situation, rather than muscle the technique along, you should wait for him to release pressure while making his next move.

1 Kid has turned to the turtle and Rodrigo is on his back. Notice that Rodrigo has more weight on his own knees than on Kid's back. Otherwise, Kid could simply grab the back of Rodrigo's gi and pull him forward off his back.

2 Kid steps out to the left, hooking his inside (right) foot on the outside of Rodrigo's left thigh. He then plants his right arm and props up his body and shoots his left knee under his body as he pushes off with his right leg, moving his hips away from Rodrigo and creating the necessary space for a complete rotation.

3 As his body rotates clockwise (caused by the momentum of his shooting left leg), Kid uses his right arm to grab Rodrigo's right arm on the outside of the elbow, and pulls him forward. To complete the closed guard, Kid closes his legs around Rodrigo's waist. Notice that Kid's right foot hook remained in place throughout the move, preventing Rodrigo from moving to the left until Kid has his buttocks on the ground.

CLOSED GUARD TECHNIQUES

The closed guard is the first barrier in ground fighting. Because your opponent is trapped between your legs, you have control and can take your time executing submissions. Remember, in addition to moving your hips from side to side, controlling your opponent's elbows and constantly breaking his posture are the keys to success in the closed guard. Keep him off balance by using your legs to assist in breaking up his posture and by attacking his neck and arms.

Notice that in this book, we consider closed guard even when the legs are not locked behind the opponent's back so long as one can easily re-lock the legs.

Breaking the Posture

As you probably already know by now, one of the keys to maintaining the closed guard and being able to attack from it is to constantly break your opponent's posture. Many times, the battle for control and posture is won or lost on small details like proper technique and grip control.

In the introduction, we briefly demonstrated a few ways to break your opponent's posture, but because the point is so crucial, we'll further elaborate on it here. In the next few techniques, we'll show several more ways to break the posture and possibly, in the process, get a submission. Remember that you need to use your entire body connected together to achieve the best results, so don't just use your arms or just your legs — use your entire body!

It's not uncommon for your opponent to use a defensive posture and close himself up, placing his hands on your belt or chest and his elbows closed around your hips. He might be resting or waiting for the fight to end. Here is a great way to end this stalemate and a great set-up for the omoplata.

1 Kid has Rodrigo in the closed guard. Rodrigo's chest is down and tight against Kid's chest, while his elbows are closed against the hips.

2 With his right hand, Kid drives Rodrigo to the left by pushing the left side of his face. At the same time, Kid opens his legs, coiling the right and driving his thigh under Rodrigo's armpit. Kid then places his right foot on Rodrigo's left hip, pushing off with it and escaping his hips to the right. Notice that Kid still keeps his right stiff arm against Rodrigo's face. At this point, Kid can attack Rodrigo's left arm with the omoplata, although the main point, breaking the defensive posture, is accomplished.

Sometimes, your opponent will simply get ahead of you and gain the proper posture. In this example, Rodrigo has his right arm forward, gripping Kid's collars together. The left hand is back grabbing the belt and pressing it down controlling the hips. His back is straight, head is up and his eyes are looking forward. To break Rodrigo's posture, Kid will have to resort to a little trickery.

1 Kid has Rodrigo in the closed guard. Rodrigo has perfect posture: his right arm is posted forward and the hand grips both collars. His left hand grabs Kid's belt and presses it down, pinning the hips. Notice Rodrigo's back, head, and eye posture.

2 Kid reaches down with both of his hands and holds his collars, just below Rodrigo's right hand.

3 Kid pulls his collars apart, opening them and breaking Rodrigo's grip. At the same time, he pulls his legs up driving Rodrigo's torso forward as he falls over Kid. Kid then wraps his arms tightly around Rodrigo's right arm and head, keeping him close. From here, Kid can initiate a variety of attacks and sweeps (i.e. the Ezequiel choke, reaching his back, etc).

In this case, Rodrigo is in another defensive posture, closing his legs and elbows tightly against Kid's hips and eliminating any room for movement. In this situation, bridging is extremely effective.

1 Kid has Rodrigo in the closed guard. Rodrigo has his knees and elbows tightly closed, trapping Kid's hips. Kid wants to break Rodrigo's position, regain movement and engage in the fight.

2 Kid plants his arms over his head and drops his feet to the ground, pushing off them and bridging his body. This throws Rodrigo back and, if he doesn't counter by leaning forward, he'll be reversed backwards.

A

B

C

3 When he feels Rodrigo pushing back against his hips, Kid quickly brings his legs back and drives Rodrigo's torso forward, causing Rodrigo to fall over him. Kid can also bring his knees back over and to the side, putting Rodrigo off balance.

Another great attack to break this defensive posture – your opponent's legs and elbows closed tightly against your hips, eliminating any space for movement – is shown here. This option is a perfect set up for the spider guard.

1 Kid has Rodrigo in the closed guard. Rodrigo's knees and elbows are closed tightly, trapping Kid's hips. Kid wants to move and engage in the fight, so he opens his guard, plants his feet on the mat and places his hands on Rodrigo's biceps.

2 Kid bridges up to his left, using his right hand to post and keep Rodrigo's left arm back. As Kid drops his back from the bridge, his right arm brace creates the space for his right leg to move in front of Rodrigo's left arm. Kid places his right shin on Rodrigo's left biceps and is ready to fight.

In this case, Kid managed to place his feet on Rodrigo's hips. In response, Rodrigo came in tightly, bringing his hips forward and close to Kid while pressing his elbows snugly against his knees. In this position, Kid doesn't have enough room to move his hips sideways.

1 Kid has his feet on Rodrigo's hips. Rodrigo is pressed tightly against Kid, with his hips forward and his elbows and knees pressing against each other.

A

B

C

2 Kid pushes off with his feet and bridges up. He places his right hand on Rodrigo's left biceps and posts the arm to keep it away as his hips come back down from the bridge. At this point, Kid has a couple options. He can coil his right leg, bringing the knee in front of Rodrigo's arm and pressing the shin against the biceps. Or, as he does here, he can escape his hips to the left and be in the perfect position to attack Rodrigo's right arm with an omoplata.

This is another alternative for the same problem. The advantage to this option is that it creates distance between you and your opponent's head and chest, setting up either the butterfly guard or the scissor sweep. We'll pick up from Kid bridging.

1 Kid bridges up, pushing off Rodrigo's hips with his feet.

2 Kid posts his left hand on Rodrigo's left shoulder and pushes the forearm against Rodrigo's throat. As he drops from his bridge, Kid escapes his hips backwards and to the left, while turning his body to the right. He is in a great position for initiating the scissor sweep or placing hooks for the butterfly guard.

Closed Guard Attacks

Regardless of your technical abilities and mastery of defensive techniques, you cannot realistically say that your guard is complete without attacking options. Submissions and sweeps are important keys to keeping your opponent challenged and under mental pressure that will lead him to make technical mistakes. If your opponent is not concerned about the threat of a submission or a reversal he can simply concentrate on the guard passing.

By having a solid combination of submissions and sweeps you will be able to not only control your opponent but also reverse the situation and achieve a quick end to a match via a submission.

Your opponent might try to break your guard by grabbing your belt and jamming the points of his elbows against the inside of your thigh. The pressure can be excruciating. Stuck in this position, many people simply try to resist the pain or give up and open their guard. This sweep is a much better option.

1 Rodrigo has Kid in the closed guard. Kid grabs Rodrigo's belt with both hands and pushes his elbows against the inside of Rodrigo's thighs, causing tremendous pain.

2 To avoid this painful pressure, Rodrigo quickly opens his legs, moves them over Kid's arms and closes them, locking Kid's arms in place. **Expert tip:** Don't open the legs too wide as the move needs to be quick to catch the opponent off guard.

3 With his right hand, Rodrigo grabs Kid's pants at the left knee. He then twists his hips to the right as he lifts Kid's leg, sweeping him to the left. Notice, because Kid's arms are trapped and he cannot brace to stop the sweep, Rodrigo can sweep to either side. If he had wanted to sweep to the right, he would simply use his left hand to grab Kid's right pants.

One quick way to create havoc in anyone's posturing battle is to apply a wristlock on the forward bracing arm. Even if the submission fails, your opponent will be very careful and jumpy when grabbing your collar, making it a lot easier to break his posture.

1 Kid has Rodrigo in the closed guard. With his right hand, Rodrigo grabs both sides of Kid's collar, posting it to establish his position. With his left hand, Rodrigo grabs Kid's belt to control his hips. If Kid doesn't respond, Rodrigo could open his guard.

2 Kid cups both of his hands behind Rodrigo's right elbow and pulls it towards his chest. At the same time, he sits up towards Rodrigo's right side, pressing his chest against Rodrigo's wrist for the wristlock.
Expert tip: By bringing his shoulders in and curving his chest, Kid traps Rodrigo's hand so he can't escape the lock. Kid sits to the side of the posting arm so that he can bend Rodrigo's wrist.

After a wrist lock, or even an attempted wrist lock, your opponent will quickly release his grip on your collar. Take advantage of this! Either go to his side or back, and then choke him.

1 Kid has Rodrigo in the closed guard. With his right arm, Rodrigo grips and posts Kid's collar. Kid's left hand grips Rodrigo's right sleeve at the wrist. He initiates the wrist lock by reaching for Rodrigo's elbow with both hands while sitting up.

2 Rodrigo quickly releases his grip on the collar, leaving his right arm loose. Taking advantage of this, Kid pulls the arm across his body with his right hand, simultaneously pulling Rodrigo's torso forward with his legs. Kid pushes Rodrigo's right arm as far to the right as possible, allowing him to slide his hips to the left and reach Rodrigo's back. **Expert tip**: It's extremely important that Kid continues to push Rodrigo's right arm to the right. This prevents him from pulling it out and regaining posture while giving Kid opportunity to press his chest against Rodrigo's shoulder, taking away the space for Rodrigo's arm to come back out . Kid reaches around Rodrigo's head with his left arm and uses the right hand to deliver Rodrigo's right collar to his left hand. Kid pulls up on the collar with his left hand as he slides his right arm behind Rodrigo's head for the choking pressure.

2 Reverse Notice how Kid's chest is glued to Rodrigo's right shoulder, eliminating the space Rodrigo needs to remove his arm. Also note how Kid uses the right hand with the arm under Rodrigo's right arm to deliver the collar to his left hand. The choking motion is shown here; the left hand pulling the collar, the right arm adding pressure by sliding behind the head.

While the cross collar choke is one of the most basic chokes in all Jiu-Jitsu, it's also one of the most effective. A lot of fighters overlook it because it's so simple, thinking, "Everyone knows it! It can't be useful." The truth is it can put your opponent in great immediate danger. Should he chose to ignore it and not pay the proper respect and attention by countering it, he will quickly be forced to submit. When he tries to counter it, his attention will be diverted and new opportunities will open up.

1 Kid has Rodrigo in the closed guard. He sets up the choke by opening Rodrigo's right lapel with his left hand and slides the right hand inside to grip it—his four fingers inside the gi, his thumb outside.

1 Detail Notice that Kid intentionally holds Rodrigo's lapel open with the left hand pulling it down . This allows him to easily slide and move his right hand in and up along his hand's crease between the index finger and thumb. **Expert tip:** For the tightest possible choke, glide your hand up the collar as far back and behind his neck as possible.

2 Kid pulls Rodrigo down by the collar with his right hand, keeping him from posturing up. Kid then opens his left hand (the four fingers pointing together), slides it under his right arm and grips Rodrigo's left collar. Notice, in both grips, his four fingers are inside the lapel while his thumbs remain out. Kid continues to slide his left hand up Rodrigo's collar, trying to get as close to his right hand as possible, ideally bringing his two hands into contact behind Rodrigo's head.

3 Kid applies the choke by pulling his elbows down toward the mat, forcing Rodrigo's head down towards his chest, and curling his wrists as if he wanted to see the knuckles. Kid uses his legs to help pull Rodrigo's torso close as well, adding pressure to the choke

A

B

C

4 **Variation** This is a good variation if you have less space under your arm. Kid opens his left hand, the palm facing up, and grabs Rodrigo's gi near the left shoulder. He applies the same choking motion by bringing his elbows to the ground and pulling Rodrigo's head to his chest.

Expert choke Details:

Incorrect A Notice how the wider side of Kid's forearm presses against Rodrigo's neck. It's much better to use a narrower part of the arm—the narrower the pressing object, the stronger and more effective the choke. Think of it as a knife cutting through an object. You always cut with the sharper, narrower edge, not the wide one.

Correct A Notice how Kid's right forearm touches the top of Rodrigo's collarbone so that the narrower, blade-like part of his arm presses against Rodrigo's neck.

Incorrect B Don't choke by opening your elbows out. Not only is the pressure weaker, but your opponent can easily counter the choke by pushing your elbows in and lifting up his head.

Correct B Always choke by bringing your elbows to the ground and pulling your opponent's head to your chest. Expand your chest using the chest muscles to add pressure

Incorrect C Make sure you don't have your wrist bent out, which will reduce the pressure. Furthermore, in this picture, Kid is incorrectly pressing against the neck with the wide part of his forearm.

Correct C Use the narrow part of your forearm to press against the neck and curl your wrist as if you wanted to see your knuckles – pull the gi as if you're wringing a towel. This will make your wrist bend inwards and add extra power to your forearm's pressure. The wringing motion alone can tighten the collar enough to choke most people.

The arm-lock from the closed guard is the perfect compliment to the cross collar choke. While they're technically independent from each other, one will perfectly set up the other. In this case, to develop the good habit of using them together, Kid initiates the arm-lock from the previous position: with his right hand inside Rodrigo's right collar.

1 Kid has Rodrigo in the closed guard. His right hand is grabbing far up Rodrigo's right collar, while his left controls Rodrigo's right sleeve near the wrist. Kid will attack the right arm.

2 Kid unlocks his legs and coils the left (on the same side as the targeted arm), placing the foot on Rodrigo's right hip. He then pushes off with it, traps Rodrigo's right arm by closing his left knee, and escapes his hips to the left, toward the targeted arm. Kid slides his right leg up and towards Rodrigo's armpit, ideally placing his calf over Rodrigo's left shoulder blade, and presses down on Rodrigo's back. Notice that Kid's torso moved to the right as his hips shifted to the left. Also, notice that Kid drove his right heel towards the ground to maintain pressure on Rodrigo's back preventing Rodrigo from arching his back and regain posture.

2 Detail

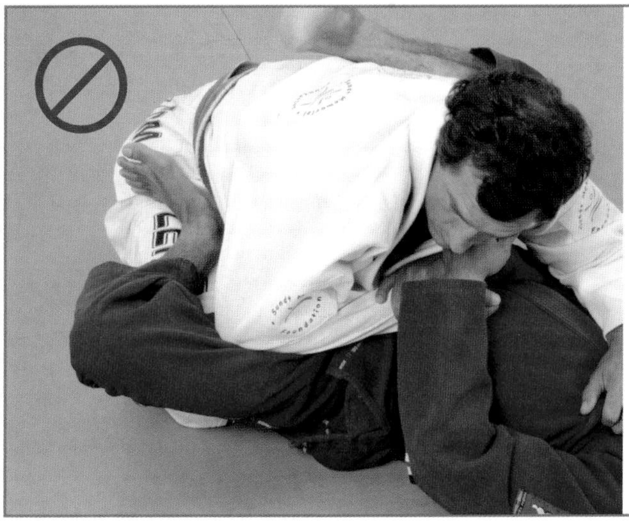

Incorrect A Kid's knee is pointing out and away from Rodrigo's side, leaving ample space for Rodrigo to pull out his elbow.

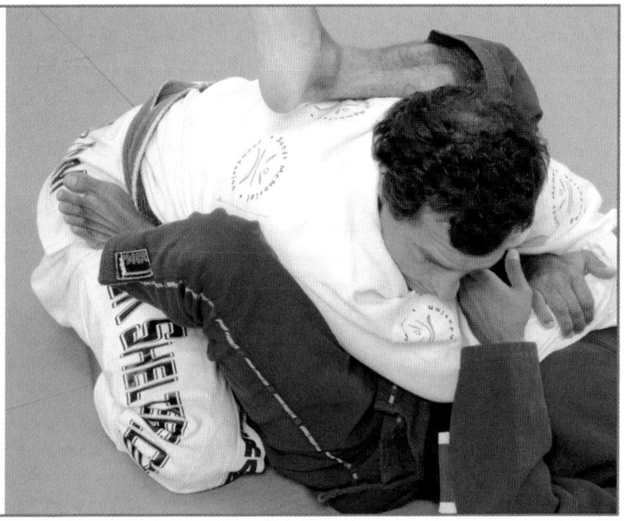

Correct A Notice how Kid's left knee is pushing against Rodrigo's shoulder, reducing open space and locking the arm.

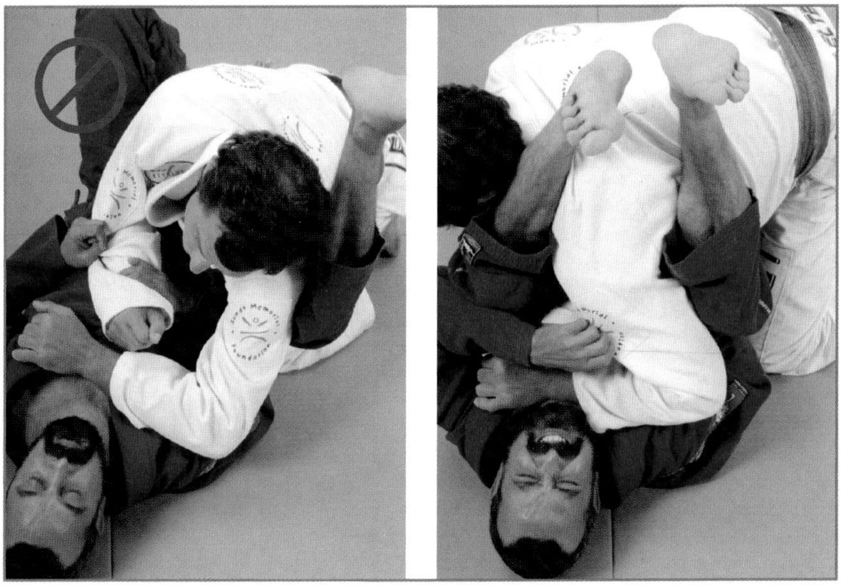

Incorrect B Kid's right leg is too low and he doesn't rotate his torso to the right, allowing Rodrigo to lean forward, get on top and stack Kid's legs.

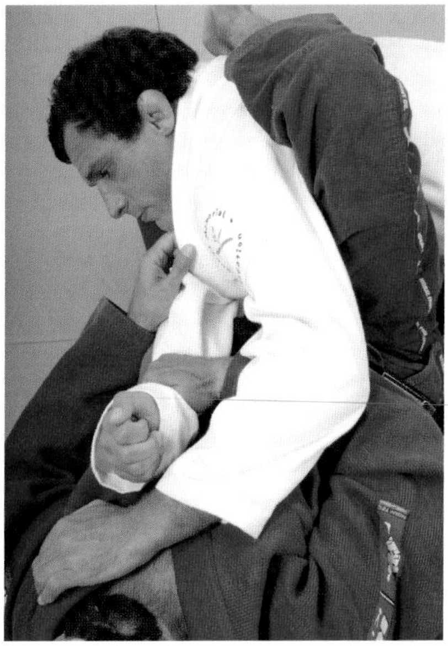

Correct B Kid's right calf is locked over and pushing down on Rodrigo's left shoulder. This forces him to lean to the right and prevents him from raising his torso.

Correct Use your leg to keep pressure on your opponent's hips. This will protect you from being stacked.

3 Kid loops his left leg around Rodrigo's head, pressing down with both heels as he lifts his hips, hyperextending Rodrigo's elbow. Notice that Kid never releases his arm grip and, in this step, grabs it with both hands. **Expert tip:** Make sure the thumb on your opponent's locked arm is pointing up, ensuring that the elbow is locked in the proper position to be hyperextended. Trap the elbow between your hips, or the arm-lock will fail. Press your knees in while keeping your legs parallel to each other, adding greater pressure and tightness.

A

B

C

Incorrect If you cross the feet, make sure you don't open your knees wide. The increased space will allow your opponent to pull out his arm.

Expert tip: Ways to Control the Arm

A Kid's right hand controls Rodrigo's right wrist; his left hand is inside Rodrigo's left collar. Advantage: Kid can easily switch between the choke and the arm-lock. Also, the left hand pulls down on the collar, preventing Rodrigo from pulling away. Disadvantage: less control over the arm.

B Kid's right hand controls Rodrigo's right wrist; his left hand grips Rodrigo's right sleeve above the elbow. Advantage: Strong control over Rodrigo's arm. Disadvantage: No options for a neck attack.

C Kid's left hand controls Rodrigo's right wrist; his right hand reaches over Rodrigo's right arm, grabbing the elbow. Advantage: This has the best arm control. Good option for reaching the back with an arm drag. Disadvantage: Too much commitment to the arm-lock alerts the opponent to the upcoming danger. Because it's harder for you to switch to another move, your opponent will be more aware of your plans and have time to focus on his main objective: escaping the arm-lock.

This is another basic but great attack from the guard. While the triangle compliments both the arm-lock and choke, it works particularly well with the arm-lock. As the opponent defends against one, the other will open up. While there are many ways to set up the triangle, the basic starting point is always the same; have one of your opponent's arms and head between your legs. When you end up in this position – whether accidentally or intentionally – you need to take advantage of it.

1 Rodrigo has Kid in the closed guard. Kid gets caught with his right arm inside Rodrigo's legs, while his left arm is under Rodrigo's right leg. This might have happened as Kid was trying to open the guard, or if he attempted a guard pass with improper posture. Regardless, opportunity for the triangle is there. Rodrigo controls Kid's right lapel with his right hand and, with his left, controls Kid's right sleeve at the elbow.

2 Rodrigo coils his left leg and places the foot on Kid's right hip. Pushing off with it, Rodrigo raises his hips up and to the left as he loops his right leg over Kid's left shoulder. Rodrigo closes his knees together, locking Kid's head and right arm. Rodrigo then bends his right leg down, pushing his heel towards the mat, and applies pressure on Kid's neck with the back of his right calf. Rodrigo maintains the grip on Kid's right arm; if he releases it, Kid could pull the arm out and avoid the triangle.

3 Rodrigo continues to press his foot against Kid's hip. He shifts his torso right and grabs his own right ankle with his left hand. Kid is now trapped inside the triangle and can't regain posture. This allows Rodrigo to release his left foot and loop the leg over his right foot locking the figure 4 for the triangle. Notice that Rodrigo continues to grip his ankle until he can lock his left leg over it and set the triangle. Kid's right arm and head are now trapped inside the lock.

4 With both hands, Rodrigo pulls Kid's right arm across his body until the elbow is past Kid's head. Rodrigo then releases Kid's arm and applies pressure on the triangle; he pulls Kid's head down with both hands squeezing his knees together at the same time.

Triangle Expert tips:

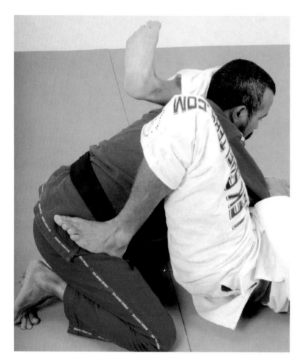

A It is extremely important that Rodrigo continues to press his left foot against Kid's right hip. This prevents Kid from moving closer, regaining posture by straightening his back, or stacking Rodrigo's legs over his shoulders.

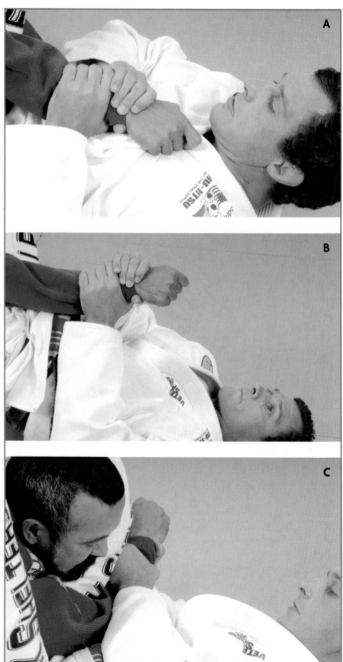

B Often, your opponent will grab your collar in an effort to stop his arm from crossing over. To counter this, take his wrist with both hands and do a couple bridge bumps up and down with your hips to break his grip. Once he releases the grip, pull his arm across and continue the move.

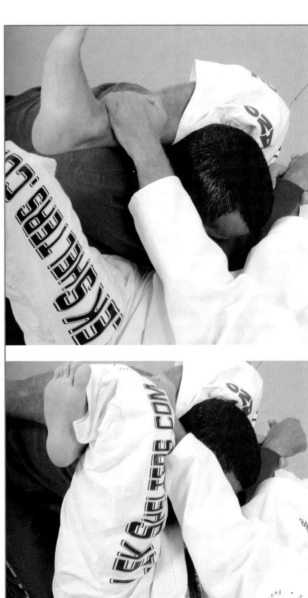

Incorrect C Grabbing the toes and locking the left leg over the end of the right foot. This is a weak lock, and a dangerous position for your underlying foot. If your opponent postures up by straightening his back, the pressure on your foot will either make you submit, or even break your foot.

Correct D Make sure that you not only hold your ankle, but keep the toes pointing up during your grip until you lock the legs.

One of the best set-ups for the triangle is simply to push your opponent's arm in while looping your leg around it. The key here is to control his wrist while not holding it so tight that you will tip off your next move. Grab the wrist somewhat lightly and, in one move, push the wrist in and loop your leg over his arm.

1 Rodrigo has Kid in the closed guard. Kid's right arm is in front; the hand grips Rodrigo's lapel and presses down on the chest to keep him from sitting up. His left hand controls Rodrigo's hips, also pressed down. Rodrigo sets up the triangle by grabbing Kid's left wrist with his right hand.

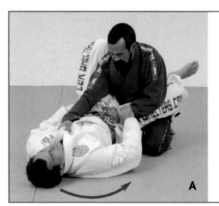  

| A | B | C |

2 Rodrigo coils his left leg and places the foot on Kid's right hip. He pushes off it, shifting his hips slightly up and to the left as he locks Kid's right arm by pressing his left knee against Kid's shoulder. Then, in one move, Rodrigo shifts his hips further to the left, opens his right leg wide and pushes Kid's left arm in. He loops his right leg around the arm until it's locked over Kid's left shoulder. Notice, as Rodrigo's hip went to the left, his torso shifted to the right, putting him in the proper angle for the triangle.

2 Expert tips:

Incorrect Rodrigo's foot is not on the hip, allowing Kid to lean forward and stack him.

Correct Rodrigo keeps his left foot pressed against Kid's right hip as he raises his hips.

3 Rodrigo grabs his right ankle with his left hand. He then loops the left leg over the right ankle, locks it and sets the triangle.

A   B   C

3 **Expert tip:** To break Kid's right handed grip on Rodrigo's collar, Rodrigo grabs the wrists with both arms and straightens his body by bridging up. On the way down, Rodrigo pulls Kid's arm across his body.

The omoplata, also known as the shoulder lock, is one of the great closed guard attacks. It compliments both the triangle and the arm-lock perfectly. Transitioning between each of them will create a formidable set of attacks that will greatly confuse and create extreme danger to your opponents. While the start-ups are different they compliment each other quite well. The key to the omoplata is having the opponent's arm open and the wrist outside the torso. To reach this position, you can open your opponent's wrist and spin your body in the direction of the arm until you can loop you leg around the arm.

1 Rodrigo has Kid in the closed guard. Kid's left hand grips Rodrigo's lapel. Kid plants his right arm on the ground and pushes off it to regain posture. Notice that Rodrigo's hands are controlling Kid's elbows and are ready to break his posture again.

A   B   C

2 As Kid attempts to raise his torso, Rodrigo pulls Kid's elbows forward, breaking his posture and making him lean forward on top of Rodrigo's chest. Kid's right arm opens up and Rodrigo begins to attack it. He coils his right leg and places the foot on Kid's left hip. Then, pushing off with it, he moves his hips right, pulls Kid's elbow further forward and, spins his torso to his left as far as he can go while looping the left leg around Kid's right arm. Notice that Rodrigo closes his right knee around Kid's left shoulder, taking away any space for Kid to escape. Rodrigo presses his left heel down and towards the ground, pushing his calf against Kid's back to prevent an upward posture.

3 Rodrigo continues to move his torso left until his head is next to Kid's right knee. Notice that Rodrigo's body is now parallel to Kid's. Rodrigo plants his right foot on the mat and grabs Kid's belt with his left hand. Rodrigo's left elbow is down and tight against his body, preventing Kid from rolling forward and escaping the submission. Rodrigo's right hand controls Kid's right arm. Rodrigo reaches back with his right leg, planting the foot on the mat. Pushing off the right foot, Rodrigo kicks his left leg forward as he moves his hips to the right, forcing Kid flat on the mat. Rodrigo coils his right leg, sitting up forcing Kid's right arm to rotate around his shoulder for the submission. If Kid's shoulder has more range, Rodrigo can simply continue to rotate his body clockwise and further torque Kid's arm around the shoulder.

3 Detail

Correct It's very important that Rodrigo's left hand correctly grips Kid's belt. The palm of his hand faces up and his elbow is kept tightly down against Kid's hips. Rodrigo pulls the belt down and forces Kid's hips in place; this keeps Kid from raising his torso and countering the move.

Incorrect Notice that Rodrigo's elbow is open and his palm is facing down. There's no pressure, allowing Kid to easily raise his torso and defend himself.

Another classic attack from the closed guard is the kimura. The kimura is very similar to the omoplata. They both attack the shoulder joint and they both begin when the opponent's arm is wide of his torso. But unlike the omoplata, which requires you to escape your hips and wrap your leg around your opponent's arm, the kimura entails sitting up and controlling the wrist. This is a perfect attack if your opponent braces on an arm that he's planted forward on the mat.

1 Kid has Rodrigo in the closed guard. Rodrigo braces with his right arm, either to gain posture or keep balance.

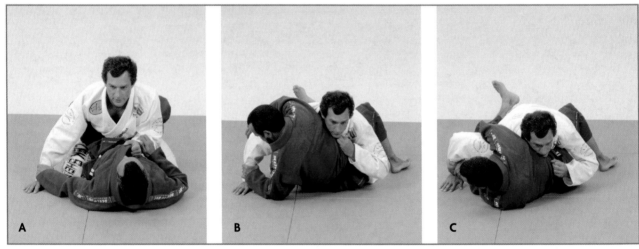

2 Seeing the opportunity for the kimura, Kid immediately seizes the chance. Kid grabs Rodrigo's wrist with his left hand, locking it in place. He opens his legs and plants his right foot on the mat. Pushing off the right foot he sits up and turns his torso to the left as his hips slide to the right, allowing him to reach his right arm around Rodrigo's arm above the elbow until he can grab his own left wrist, locking in the kimura hold.

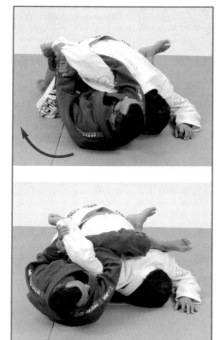

3 With Rodrigo's arm locked, Kid uses his legs to move his hips completely to the other side. Kid switches feet, planting the left foot. He pushes off with it, sliding his hips and body to the left, forcing Rodrigo's left arm up and around in a clockwise motion. Kid torques the shoulder joint as if he wanted Rodrigo's hand to touch his right ear. It is crucial that Kid uses his body movement from right to left to torque Rodrigo's arm. This is particularly true when fighting a stronger opponent; while he might be able to resist a simple arm push, it's much harder for him to resist the entire body's forcing the arm over. Kid loops his left leg over Rodrigo's back, preventing him from somersaulting over his left shoulder and escaping the pressure. Notice that Kid's right leg is not flat on the mat but bent up. The calf and ankle prevent Rodrigo from jumping over the leg and escaping the pressure. **Expert tip:** For greater torque, keep your opponent's elbow glued to your chest. The further away his elbow is from your chest, the less pressure you can apply to his shoulder. This is particularly important against fighters with great flexibility and a wide range of motion in their joints.

3 **Incorrect A** Kid doesn't loop his left leg over Rodrigo's back. Rodrigo escapes the submission by rolling forward over his shoulder and reaching side control.

3 **Incorrect B** Kid leaves his leg flat on the mat, allowing Rodrigo to step over it and, by using the same grips as Kid, placing Kid in the kimura.

This is a great reversal from the closed guard. It can be used in a variety of ways to reverse the position and mount your opponent. The general rule for the cross over sweep: have your opponent leaning back and control one side of his body, preventing him from bracing and blocking the sweep. A great time to use the cross over sweep is when your opponent defends against the cross choke by posturing up. It also works well from the kimura (technique 54). When your opponent counters it, either by reaching in or putting his weight on the attacked arm, you can execute the cross over sweep. The key for this move is to use your hips to bump the opponent up and over.

1 Kid has Rodrigo in the closed guard. Rodrigo is leaning back to defend Kid's choke attempt. Kid follows Rodrigo's the direction of body lean, as he begins to sit up.

2 Kid plants his left hand behind him on the mat. He opens his legs and plants the right foot on the mat next to Rodrigo's left leg. Pushing off with it, he lifts his hips while reaching his right arm across his body and wrapping it around Rodrigo's right arm. At this point, Rodrigo's right side is blocked: Kid's right arm trapping Rodrigo's right arm, his left leg trapping the right leg (Kid's left foot is planted next to Rodrigo's right foot). Notice that Kid's hip are tightly connected with Rodrigo's hips.

3 Kid continues to push off with his right foot as he uses his hips to force Rodrigo to his right, finishing with a mount. Notice that Kid is reversed on the blocked side (in this case the right), ending up at 45° angle from where he started. It would have been far more difficult to try to force Rodrigo backward over the legs.

If you can connect multiple attack options, you will greatly increase your chances of success with any one of them. If your opponent counters one attack, you will immediately have another move prepared, which will quicken your reaction time, giving him less time to counter. The guillotine, kimura and cross over sweep are a perfect trio for this. When your opponent counters the kimura by leaning over, you use the sweep, and if he postures forward to counter the sweep, hit him with the guillotine. Remember, since the three techniques are all interconnected, if Rodrigo tries to counter the guillotine, he'll become vulnerable to one of the other two attacks.

1 In reaction to Kid's cross over sweep, Rodrigo leans forward, forces his hips down, straightens his back and lifts his head up, exposing his neck for the guillotine.

2 Pushing off with his feet and left arm, Kid slides his hips back and wraps his right arm around Rodrigo's neck. It is extremely important to slide your hips back in order to create space between you and your opponent's chest. This allows you to reach with your arm and wrap it around his neck.

3 While still sitting with his hips back, Kid grabs his right wrist with his left hand; all five fingers are in a hook grip under the wrist. Kid cinches the noose around Rodrigo's head, bringing the right elbow in and closing any space between his forearm and Rodrigo's throat. He then wraps his legs around Rodrigo's body for the closed guard and leans back, applying pressure to the guillotine by pulling his right forearm up with his left hand and, by extending his legs, pushing Rodrigo's body away. It is very important for Kid to have a tight noose around Rodrigo's head *before* he leans back and applies the pressure. If he doesn't, Rodrigo's head could slip out of the grip.

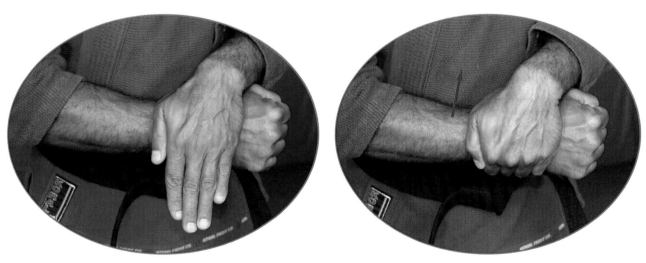

3 Detail Notice how Kid grabs his right wrist with his left hand. All the fingers cup under the wrist together. The direction of the choking pressure is up.

The key-lock is a great attack from the guard that is often under-used. Opportunities to use the key-lock actually appear quite frequently—so be looking for them. In this case Kid breaks Rodrigo's posture and uses the key-lock as Rodrigo fights to regain control of his grip

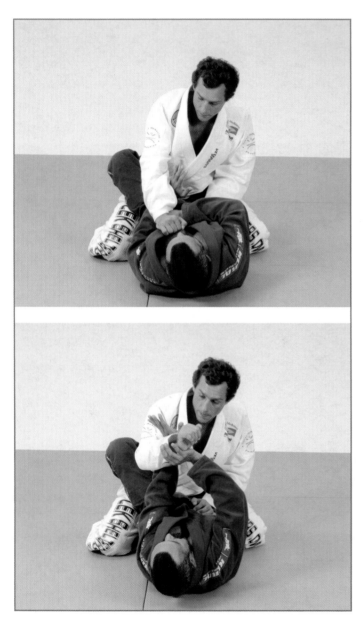

1 Kid has Rodrigo in the closed guard. Rodrigo's right hand is forward, controlling Kid's collar and keeping him from sitting up. Kid wants to break Rodrigo's control and posture. He slips his right hand, the palm facing up, under Rodrigo's right wrist and grabs it. At the same time, Kid slides his left forearm under Rodrigo's right forearm. Then, in one motion, Kid pushes up with the right hand and drives the left arm forward and up, breaking Rodrigo's grip on the collar. Kid maintains control over Rodrigo's wrist with the right hand.

A

B

C

2 Kid pushes Rodrigo's wrist up with his right hand as he circles his left hand around the top of Rodrigo's arm, until he can lock it on his own right wrist securing the key-lock grip on Rodrigo's right arm. Kid applies pressure on Rodrigo's shoulder by driving Rodrigo's arm to the left, in a counter-clockwise direction.

While the cross choke from the guard is extremely effect, it's also very common. This means that a lot of opponents will know how to defend against it. Here, Kid shows a few counter-attacks to some common defenses.

1 Kid has Rodrigo in the closed guard. Kid's right hand is inside Rodrigo's collar and he's ready to initiate the cross choke attack. Rodrigo pushes off with both arms and straightens his back to gain posture and break Kid's grip.

2 Kid supports himself on his left arm as he sits up, turns his torso to the left and, with his right hand, re-establishes his grip on Rodrigo's collar reaching as far in as he can. Kid opens his legs and places his left foot on Rodrigo's right hip.

3 Pushing off with the left foot, Kid lies back and pivots his torso to the right. This gives him a better angle to grab Rodrigo's left collar with his left hand, completing the choke.

4 Having secured his grip, Kid re-centers his body and applies the choke, pulling his elbow down to the mat and expanding his chest. You should bring your opponent's head to your chest as if you were hugging him Remember, to find tune your choke, use the expert tips from position 49.

5 A typical counter: As soon as Kid establishes his grip, Rodrigo leans forward and props his hands under Kid's elbows, pushing them up and preventing Kid from applying proper pressure. Kid pushes off with his legs and slides his body back, forcing Rodrigo to lean forward achieving a better angle to apply the choking pressure.

A

B

C

6 Another common counter: Rodrigo crosses his arms over Kid's arms. This makes a frame with the arms, creating distance for Rodrigo to prop his head up and keep Kid's elbows from reaching the mat. In this case, Kid places both feet on Rodrigo's hips and pushes off with them, extending his legs and sitting up. As in the previous example, this forces Rodrigo to lean forward and into the choke. The pressure of the legs pushing Rodrigo's hips away will also add to the choke's pressure.

7 If Rodrigo still resists, Kid sits up, pushes his hips further away and leans back, forcing Rodrigo flat on his stomach and falling further into the choke's pressure. Notice, from this position, Kid can easily hook his right foot under Rodrigo's left hip and sweep him to the left. He would end up choking and mounted on Rodrigo.

The scissor sweep is one of the most basic and effective sweeps in Brazilian Jiu-Jitsu. By scissoring your legs and pulling your opponent over the top of your body, you'll be able to sweep him, finishing in the mounted position and, if executed in a competition, earning you six points (two for the sweep and four for the mount). The first key to a good scissor sweep is to keep your shin on your opponent's hips, blocking him from coming too close. Remember, don't drop your knees too far to the mat. This would allow him to drop his hips on your legs, rendering them ineffective as blocks by pinning them to the mat and easily passing your guard. The second key: pull your opponent's torso up and towards you, transferring his weight onto your legs and making him much lighter.

1 Kid has Rodrigo in the closed guard. Kid grabs Rodrigo's right lapel with his right hand; his fingers on the outside and thumbs inside (for a variation of the grip to be used in a combination attack later) pointing up. Kid's left hand controls Rodrigo's right sleeve at the wrist.

2 Kid opens his legs and plants the right foot on the mat next to Rodrigo's left side, pushes off it escaping his hips to the right and slightly away from Rodrigo. Kid slides his right knee in front of Rodrigo's hips until he can hook the foot on the outside of Rodrigo's left hip. At the same time, Kid drops his left leg, bent at the knee, and places it on the mat next to Rodrigo's right leg.

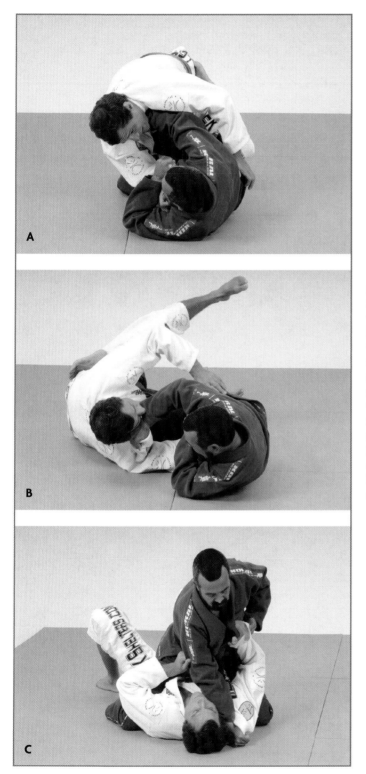

3 Kid pulls Rodrigo's collar with his right hand, forcing Rodrigo's weight forward and against Kid's right shin. As soon as Kid feels Rodrigo's weight against his shin, he scissors his legs, kicking his right foot forward while bringing in the left heel. The left heel breaks Rodrigo's right knee brace while his right foot pushes Rodrigo's hip over, completing the sweep. **Expert tip:** It's important that Kid keeps some distance between his and Rodrigo's hips. That way, his right leg won't be too cocked. If his right heel is close to or touching his right buttock, then he's too close and the sweep will fail. Also, it's important that Kid doesn't point his right knee down towards the mat. He needs to keep it slightly up so that his shin is as close to parallel to the ground as possible, otherwise, Rodrigo can drive his hips down and kill the legs effectiveness by pinning them down to the mat.

Having your opponent in the closed guard allows you to attempt your attacks and submissions with a deliberate pace. Of course, as previously stated, you constantly need to break your opponent's posture if you want to maintain the closed guard. This is also the key to attacking the opponent, particularly with chokes. The Ezequiel is a sneaky and extremely effective choke from the closed guard. **Expert tip:** Since a smart opponent is always alert to chokes, the key is to slip the choking hand in front of their neck. You can do this by holding your opponent's head so close to you that he struggles to pull it away to regain posture. As he tries to pry his head away, you may be able to get a hand in.

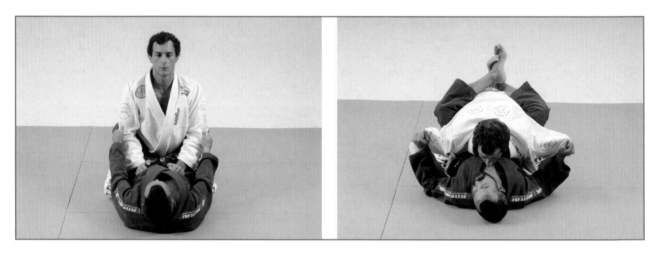

1 Kid has Rodrigo in the closed guard. Rodrigo is about to reach the perfect posture to pass Kid's guard; both arms are semi-extended, while his hands grip Kid's belt. Kid wants to break Rodrigo's posture before he has time to settle his position. Kid grabs Rodrigo's sleeves at the elbows and pulls them out and towards his head, taking away Rodrigo's ability to brace. At the same time, he brings his legs in and forces Rodrigo's torso to drop forward.

2 Kid wraps his left arm around Rodrigo's head, keeping it close to his chest. There is a struggle here; Rodrigo plants his hands on the mat and pushes to regain his posture. Because Rodrigo is using his arms to push off the ground, he can't use them to defend his neck. This is the perfect time for Kid to attack. With his left hand, he grabs the inside of his own right sleeve

3 Kid circles his right hand around the grip and slides it under Rodrigo's chin, extending his arms to apply the choking pressure against Rodrigo's neck. **Expert tip:** Kid extends the arms by driving his right hand up (in the direction of Rodrigo's right ear) as if he wanted to touch the back of Rodrigo's neck with both of his hands.

3 **Detail** Notice Kid's grip. His left hand's fingers grab inside the sleeve, giving a secure grip that his right arm can pivot around.

Closed Guard Attack Combinations

Now that you've seen the basic attacks from the guard, we'll demonstrate how to link these techniques in relation to your opponent's reactions, creating a continuous flow of attacks. Of course, ideally you want to submit the opponent with the first attack. But, if he reacts properly, you need to be able to immediately switch to another attack. If you have a solid attack sequence, you can quickly change your attack techniques, eventually catching your opponent and submitting him. Keep two things in mind: First, don't insist on a lost position; quickly move to your next option as soon as you realize your opponent's defense is working. Second, by quickly and frequently changing back to your previous attack, you can catch your opponent. Once he believes that he's safe from your last attack, he'll change his stance and prepare for a new attack, not expecting a repeat.

Notice that each attack is linked to the previous one. Depending on your opponent's counter, you can either revert back to the previous one, or continue to the next. Again, *the crucial factor is your opponent's reaction.* Don't just progress to your next move because you're used to the pattern—you need to focus on the initial attack, progressing to your next option only once your opponent successfully neutralizes the first one.

Drill suggestion: Drill this sequence with a partner to perfect the mechanics. Eventually, try it in a sparring match and, rather than submitting the opponent with each move, allow him to escape so you can strengthen and smoothen the transition between the various attacks. After this, you should try to catch him, and apply pressure until he is almost ready to submit but don't make him submit yet. Instead, continue to switch to different attacks, improving your fluidity. By using these drills, you'll not only master different sequences and variations, but you'll also greatly improve your timing and precision. It will put you on the road to becoming a deadly submission machine.

The choke to arm lock combination is a staple of the closed guard attack. By breaking your opponent's posture and switching between the attacks, you will be able to get ahead of him and successfully submit.

1 Rodrigo has Kid in the closed guard. Rodrigo's right hand holds the inside of Kid's right collar.

2 Rodrigo grabs Kid's right elbow with his left hand and places his left foot on Kid's right hip. Rodrigo pushes off his foot, shifting his hips to the left and his torso to the right. He then releases his left hand grip and grabs Kid's left shoulder—locking the cross choke and the submission.

3 As Rodrigo switches the grip to attack the collar, Kid raises his head and torso, defending against the choke. In response, Rodrigo quickly pushes off with his left leg and slides his hips out further to the left as he presses in his left knee, trapping Kid's right arm. Rodrigo raises his right leg, placing it directly under Kid's left armpit. Notice, Rodrigo's left hand is still grabbing Kid's left shoulder, maintaining a brace to keep the shoulder at arms' length while making it easier to loop his leg in the next step. Notice that Rodrigo still has the hands ready and in position to apply the cross choke.

A

B

C

4 Rodrigo pulls his right leg up further, pressing his calf on Kid's back to make him lean to the right and, at the same time, pulls Kid's torso down with his left arm. Rodrigo moves his torso slightly to the right, looping his left leg in front of Kid's head for the arm-lock. Rodrigo extends his body, pressing the hips against Kid's elbow for the submission. **Expert tip:** If Kid had leaned forward to counter the arm lock, he would be vulnerable to a choke; Rodrigo's chose his attack because of Kid's reaction.

Sometimes the opponent manages to pull his arm from the lock. If this happens, the triangle is a good option.

1 Rodrigo applies the arm-lock to Kid's right arm. But Kid manages to pull his arm out and free his elbow. Rodrigo grips Kid's left arm with both hands.

2 Rodrigo plants his right foot on the mat, and pushes off it, moving his torso back to the center while looping his left leg around Kid's head over his right shoulder. Rodrigo continues to escape his hips to the right (torso to the left) as he presses his left calf down on Kid's neck, forcing Kid down until Rodrigo can grab his own left ankle with his right hand. Notice, at the same time, Rodrigo pulled Kid's right arm across his body with his left hand at the same time.

3 Rodrigo locks his right leg over his left ankle, finalizing the triangle.

Sometimes, when the opponent feels the triangle coming, he's able to straighten his back and posture up. In this case, you should immediately switch to the omoplata.

1 Rodrigo switches from the arm lock to the triangle, but before he can lock his legs, Kid straightens his back and postures up with his head, countering the attack.

2 With his left arm, Rodrigo pushes Kid's left arm back, bending it back at the elbow. Rodrigo then plants his left foot on the ground and pushes off with it. As he pushes, he moves his hips to the left and his head to the right, simultaneously looping his right leg around Kid's left arm and, with his right hand, grabbing Kid's belt (making sure to keep his elbows down towards the mat; see omoplata). His body is now parallel to Kid's

3 As Rodrigo continues to escape his hips to the left, he forces Kid to the mat, leans forward and applies the shoulder lock.

As soon as your opponent feels the omoplata coming, he can raise his body and keep his legs (above the knees) aligned with his torso. This is an extremely common defense that's bound to occur often. When it happens, revert back to the triangle. Again, notice that, depending on your opponent's reaction, you're able to go back and forth between two attacks.

1 As Rodrigo switches from the triangle attack to the omoplata, Kid raises his body and counters the attack.

2 Rodrigo moves his torso and hips to the left as he loops his left leg around Kid's head, pressing it over Kid's right shoulder and locking his feet together with the left leg over the right one. Rodrigo places his right foot on Kid's left hip and pushes off it, moving his (Rodrigo's) hips away and breaking Kid's posture. At the same time, he wraps his left leg over the back of Kid's neck, grabbing the ankle with his right hand and, with his left arm, pulling Kid's left arm across his body.

3 Rodrigo locks his right leg over the left ankle finalizing the triangle choke.

The scissor sweep to choke is another interesting attack combo. In the previous sequence, when Rodrigo countered Kid's first submission, Kid responded with a second one. In this case, Kid uses a sweep-submission combo: he follows a submission attempt with a sweep and a sweep attempt with a submission. If mastered and used properly, this can be an extremely effective combination, either giving a choke or a sweep. Notice, for this combo, Kid's initial cross choke grip is different; the thumb is inside and pointing down, while the fingers remain outside.

1 Kid has Rodrigo in the closed guard. Kid's right hand grabs Rodrigo's right collar, but this time, his hand is pointing down with the fingers outside the gi and the thumb inside. Kid's left hand controls Rodrigo's right sleeve at the wrist.

2 Kid turns to the left and, to set up the scissor sweep, pulls in the right knee until the shin is in front of Rodrigo's hips, while bringing his left leg down to the mat and bending it next to Rodrigo's right knee. At the same time Kid grabs Rodrigo's left lapel with the left hand. At this point, Kid has two attack options: the choke and the sweep.. Kid applies the choke. He raises his right forearm up and against Rodrigo's throat as he pulls Rodrigo's left collar with his left hand tightening the choke. Rodrigo defends the choke, using both arms to control Kid's hands. With both arms tied up defending the choke, Rodrigo can't brace, giving Kid an opening for the scissor sweep.

3 If Rodrigo decides to defend against the sweep and brace with his right arm: Rodrigo uses his left hand to push down on Kid's right elbow, relieving the pressure of Kid's forearm on his neck. As Rodrigo pushes Kid's right elbow down, Kid slides his left hand up on Rodrigo's left collar. Notice that Rodrigo's right hand is busy defending the sweep; he can't use it to block Kid's hand from establishing the grip and cinching the choke.

If you can break your opponent's posture and keep him close, many great options become possible. In the previous technique, Kid managed to sneak in an Ezequiel choke. In this series, he begins with the arm-wrap—from there a large variety of attacks can be launched. As we've said before, correctly setting up the technique is the key to success. But setting up isn't easy; completing a move is much easier than properly setting it up. In this case, the set up is breaking the opponent's posture and wrapping his arm.

Compare this combination with the previous one. You'll realize that these two attacks have similar patterns, which means you can use similar sequence and approach to other positions that you favor and are able to reach regularly. Again, in a combination series, it's always important to fully commit to each technique and really want it to succeed. You should only switch to another technique once your opponent has successfully defended your last one. Also, remember that you don't decide your next move, your opponent's escapes and reactions do. This means that you have to always be prepared and reject any preconceived notions of how your opponent will react.

1 Kid has Rodrigo in the closed guard. Rodrigo has good posture and is preparing to break and pass Kid's guard. Kid's hands are gripping Rodrigo's sleeves at the elbows. Once Rodrigo begins to move, Kid pulls Rodrigo's elbows open and drives his legs up to his head, forcing Rodrigo's torso to fall forward and onto Kid. Rodrigo plants his hands on the mat, to push off and try to regain posture. At this point, Kid has two choices. He can grab the back of Rodrigo's head, which would keep him from moving backwards, and wrap the arm. Or, he can hold Rodrigo's left shoulder with his right hand while wrapping his left arm around Rodrigo's right arm as he does here. Both approaches work well; it's completely a matter of personal preference. What is important is to keep your opponent from going back quickly otherwise you will not be able to wrap the arm. By holding the head you may be able to use the Ezequiel choke.
Expert tip: You should not hold the opponent's head and chest so close to you that you cannot slide your arm in to grab the collar. By arching your torso back a little you will allow a little space so you can easily reach with your arm.

2 Kid wraps his left arm Rodrigo's right arm above the elbow. With his right hand, Kid pulls Rodrigo's left lapel and passes it to his left hand, completely securing his grip on Rodrigo's right arm. After locking Rodrigo's right arm in place, Kid releases his right hand and moves the arm back to his head.

3 Kid then places his left foot on Rodrigo's right hip, pushing off with it and moving his hips and torso to the left. Kid moves his right leg slightly up and against Rodrigo's left side, preventing Rodrigo from jumping over and reaching side control. With his torso out wide to the left, Kid has a clear path for his right arm to grab Rodrigo's collar. He locks the hand on the right side of the collar, as close to the back of Rodrigo's neck as possible, and pulls his elbows in, applying the choke.

At times when faced with the arm-wrap and the imminent choke the opponent will try to move his torso back to create distance between his neck and the attacking hands in order to counter the choke. That is the perfect time to switch to the arm bar

1 Kid has successfully wrapped Rodrigo's right arm with his left and attacks the neck for the choke. Rodrigo leans back to escape the choking pressure

2 Pushing off his left foot, Kid turns his body further to his right and arches his torso back in a clockwise motion. He then bends his left leg, sliding the left knee over the top of Rodrigo's shoulder and presses it down against it. The combination of Kid's torso leaning back pushing Rodrigo's forearm and Kid's left thigh pressing against the back of his own left arm that is wrapped over Rodrigo's right elbow applies the pressure against Rodrigo's elbow for the arm bar. Should Rodrigo try to counter and lean back in the choke is always present since Kid does not release his hands from Rodrigo's collar

At times, a smart opponent can roll his wrist, turn his arm, bend it inward and point his elbow away from the pressure as a counter to the arm-bar. When this occurs, switch to the omoplata.

1 Rodrigo counters the arm bar by quickly turning his wrist and bending the right arm back, pointing his elbow away from the pressure.

2 Kid immediately switches to the omoplata, sliding his left hand from Rodrigo's collar to his sleeve near the right wrist while looping his left leg around Rodrigo's right arm. Kid releases his right hand from the collar, using it, along with his right foot, to turn his torso clockwise. Once Kid's head is 180 degrees from where he began and his body is parallel to Rodrigo's Kid switches with his right hand, replacing his left hand's grip on Rodrigo's right wrist. With his left hand, he grabs Rodrigo's pants at the right ankle, preventing him from escaping the pressure by rolling forward over his shoulder. Kid sits up, scoots his hips to the right and opens his left arm, extending Rodrigo's left leg and forcing him flat on the mat. By driving his hips forward, Kid torques Rodrigo's right arm around his shoulder and completes the submission.

If your wrap isn't tight enough, or your opponent is particularly strong, he might be able to counter your arm-bar by simply pulling his arm out. When this happens, the Americana is a great option.

1 As Kid adjusts for an arm-bar or choke, Rodrigo pulls his right arm out. If Kid insists on fighting against this pull, Rodrigo could possibly free his wrist and escape from the arm wrap.

2 Kid drives his left elbow down, forcing Rodrigo's elbow to bend down, and coils his leg, pressing it down and over Rodrigo's biceps. As Kid's triceps push Rodrigo's right wrist back, his elbow and thigh force Rodrigo's elbow up. This causes Rodrigo's arm to twist around his shoulder and completes the key-lock.

You opponent will often counter the arm-lock by bending his arm forward and holding your shoulder. You should respond with the triangle. For more details on the exact set-up, refer to technique 81 in the Windmill series.

1 Kid has applied the arm-wrap to Rodrigo's right arm using the previous technique sequence, where he goes for the key-lock. As Kid initiates the key-lock, Rodrigo bends his arm forward and grabs Kid's gi at the shoulder. Kid uses his right arm to fend off Rodrigo's left arm, coils his right leg in, places his right foot on the biceps and pushes Rodrigo back.

2 Rodrigo reacts by pushing forward against the pressure. Kid exploits this and shoots his right foot up, locking the leg around Rodrigo's neck as Rodrigo falls forward. Kid traps Rodrigo's right arm and head with the figure four, pulls Rodrigo's right arm across his body and, for the triangle choke, applies pressure. **Expert tip:** Make sure you create enough space when pushing your torso to the left to allow your right leg to come in. If it's hard to maneuver your leg, you probably haven't turned your torso far enough left.

At times, because the opponent is so focused on freeing the arm-wrap, he forgets about his free arm and leaves it dangling. Other times, in his effort to counter or defend an attack, the free arm will move across his body without holding on to anything. Either way, when this occurs, your opponent is vulnerable for an arm-lock.

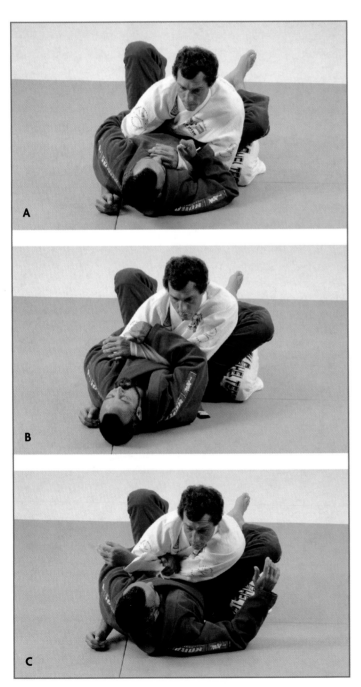

1 Kid's left arm is wrapped around Rodrigo's right; Kid's hand grips Rodrigo's left collar and traps the arm. Rodrigo's left arm is in front of Kid's chest, but for some reason – perhaps transitioning between grips – it isn't grabbing anything. Kid attacks it. He holds Rodrigo's left sleeve at the wrist with his right hand, pulling it across his body until he can reach it with his left hand. Kid then releases his grip on the collar and, with his left hand, grabs Rodrigo's left arm near the elbow. Notice that at this point, using only his left arm, Kid controls both of Rodrigo's arms.

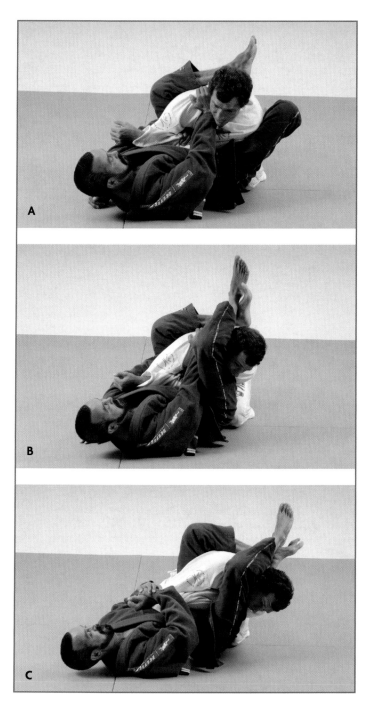

A

B

C

2 Kid places his right foot on Rodrigo's left hip, pushes off it moving his torso to the left. With his right hand, Kid grabs Rodrigo's right shoulder and stiffens his arm, preventing Rodrigo from leaning in and getting the proper angle and distance for an arm-lock. Kid then loops his right leg over Rodrigo's head locking the arm-lock. At this point, Kid releases his right hand from Rodrigo's shoulder and grabs the wrist with both hands. He extends his legs, driving his hips against Rodrigo's elbow for the submission, and hyperextends the joints.

Here, Rodrigo demonstrates an alternative way to reach the arm-wrap. In this case, rather than breaking the opponent's posture by pulling the elbows, he breaks Stefano's grips on his collar. He'll continue, as in the last technique, by forcing his opponent forward with his legs. This option works well when the opponent keeps his elbows down and close to his body. Once the wrap is successful, all the previous attacks will work. In this example, Rodrigo continues with a couple of sweeps.

1 Rodrigo has Stefano in the closed guard. Stefano has his hands on Rodrigo's collar and his elbows bent down and tight against his body. Rodrigo grips Stefano's sleeves with both his hands. Because Rodrigo only wants to break one grip at first, he grabs Stefano's right sleeve with his right hand, sliding his left hand under Stefano's right arm.

2 In one motion, Rodrigo pulls up on Stefano's sleeve, while driving his left arm entirely through the created gap and pushing the forearm against Stefano's arm to break the grip. At the same time, Rodrigo drives Stefano's torso forward with his legs as he continues to push Stefano's right wrist up and over his head and he wraps his left arm around it. Rodrigo reaches and grabs Stefano's left collar with his left hand.

A B C

3 Rodrigo opens his legs, places his left foot on Stefano's right hip and pushes off with it, moving his hips to the left. He grabs Stefano's left triceps with his right hand. Still in control of the wrap, Rodrigo slides his hips back, hooks his left foot under Stefano's right thigh and drops his right leg down.

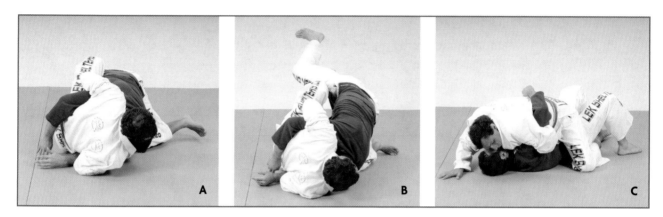

4 Rodrigo drops his head towards the mat as he pulls Stefano's left arm with his right arm. Using the momentum of his torso falling towards the ground, Rodrigo lifts Stefano's right leg with his left foot hook. At the same time, Rodrigo kicks his right leg in, scissoring Stefano's left knee from the ground to sweep Stefano to the right. **Expert tip:** Notice that since Rodrigo wants to sweep to his right side, he blocks Stefano's left arm and leg to prevent him from bracing.

5 **Optional** If Stefano, trying to resist Rodrigo's right legged scissor, puts his weight on the left knee, Rodrigo can switch, pushing the knee out with the right foot instead.

At times, when you use the arm wrap, your opponent will hold his free arm slightly away from his body. If this occurs, you should slide your arm under his and go around that side to his back. If your opponent is clever, he'll probably block the move by wrapping his own arm around your underhook, blocking your path to his back. In response, you should initiate this sweep.

1 Rodrigo has wrapped Stefano's right arm with his left, gripping the collar with his hand. Because Stefano's left arm is away from his body, Rodrigo uses his right hand to push it out slightly move and then slides his right arm under Stefano's armpit. Rodrigo moves his hips to the right as he tries to reach Stefano's back. If Stefano doesn't react, Rodrigo can continue to move around Stefano's torso until he reaches the back.

2 Stefano blocks Rodrigo's path by wrapping his left arm over Rodrigo's right arm until his hand is completely in front of Rodrigo's torso. In response, Rodrigo grabs Stefano's belt with his right hand, plants his right foot on the mat and pushes off it, sliding his hips out until he can hook his right foot under Stefano's left thigh. At the same time Rodrigo drops his left leg to the mat right next to Stefano's right knee blocking it.

3 Rodrigo drops his head to the left, pulling Stefano's right arm in with his left arm wrap while, pulling Stefano's belt with his right hand. This makes Stefano's weight move up. Then, as Rodrigo raises his right foot hook and lifts Stefano's leg, he kicks his left leg in, scissoring Stefano's right leg off the mat and sweeping him to the left. Rodrigo ends mounted on Stefano ready to apply a cross choke. Notice that Stefano cannot avoid the sweep since Rodrigo maintained control over Stefano's right arm and he scissored the right knee in.

3 Reverse Notice that Rodrigo's left leg swings in a scissor motion, moving Stefano's right knee off the mat, destroying his last brace and last defense against the sweep. If Stefano tries to avoid the scissor by putting his weight on the right knee, Rodrigo can simply change from the scissor and push the knee back with his foot.

The ankle grab works well when your opponent stands up and prepares to pass your guard. The first key to this sweep is to execute it just as he stands up and before he gains posture (hips forward and head up). The second key is to push your heels to the ground, instead of pushing them up, as you drop your hips and apply the sweep. By pushing your heels up, you will move your hips up and your power goes straight up against his chest. But, when you push the heels down, you force your hips against your opponent's pushing him back forcing the fall.

1 Kid has Rodrigo in the closed guard, but Rodrigo manages to stand up and prepares to pass Kid's guard. If Kid doesn't react, Rodrigo can break the guard and easily pass it.

2 Realizing that the position is lost, Kid opens his guard, grabs the back of Rodrigo's ankles with both hands and, drops his buttocks to the ground while keeping his legs straight.

3 Kid pushes his hips forward as he bends the legs and drives his heels down and towards the ground while still grabbing Rodrigo's ankles to prevent him from stepping back. Because Rodrigo can't step back, he falls backwards. At this point there would be a slight stalemate. Both Kid and Rodrigo have an equal position; they are both sitting down with their legs out in front.

4 In order for Kid to progress and mount Rodrigo, he uses Rodrigo's momentum from the fall. As Rodrigo's buttocks fall near the ground, Kid grabs Rodrigo's right sleeve with his right arm and gets on top, taking advantage of Rodrigo's backward momentum. Kid plants his left hand on the mat, pushing off it to help get on top of Rodrigo. Notice, Kid doesn't just get directly on top of Rodrigo, which would allow too much space and take too long. This is because he would have to prop his hips up and over Rodrigo's bent legs and then drop forward onto Rodrigo's knees. Instead, Kid circles to Rodrigo's right side and drops his left knee to the ground, forcing the leg flat on the mat and raising his body up and over the left leg until he is mounted on Rodrigo.

Many times, when you apply the ankle grab sweep, the opponent will use a straight arm to block your body and prevent you from getting top position. When this occurs, you should immediately switch to the arm-lock.

1 Using the ankle grab sweep, Kid has dropped Rodrigo to the ground. But, as he moves to the top, Rodrigo plants his right hand back and extends his left arm, places it against Kid's left shoulder and blocks him.

2 Kid wraps his right arm around Rodrigo's left arm. Kid continues to push with his left arm while driving his hips forward and to the left as if he wanted to get on top of Rodrigo. In this stalemate, Kid and Rodrigo both fight for position

3 Taking advantage of Rodrigo's extended arm, Kid turns his body to the left and loops his right leg around Rodrigo's left arm. Notice, unlike the normal arm-lock, Kid doesn't loop the leg completely over and around Rodrigo's head. Instead, he hooks the foot on top of Rodrigo's head, pressing his left shin against Rodrigo's face. Still pivoting around his left arm, Kid continues to turn his body to the left and drive his hips down and against Rodrigo's left elbow, applying the arm-lock. Because Kid hooked his foot on Rodrigo's head, rather than looping it around, Kid can drive Rodrigo's head to the mat while keeping the elbow locked in the proper position to apply the pressure. The pressure from Kid's right leg keeps Rodrigo torso flat on the ground preventing him from twisting his arm around and protecting his elbow.

A common counter against the ankle grab sweep is for the opponent to grab both collars and lean forward. In this case, you should immediately switch to the overhead sweep. The over-head sweep can be used alone, or in reaction to the opponent's counter to the ankle grab sweep. **Expert tip:** Whenever you're able to look straight up and see your opponent's head, you're in the perfect position to execute the overhead sweep. Regardless of how you end up in the position – he could just lean forward, or you might have to hop forward and under him – the key is to be under the opponent's body.

1 Kid attempts the ankle grab sweep. Rodrigo counters by grabbing Kid's collar with both of his hands and leaning forward to regain balance. Notice, at this point, Rodrigo's head is almost in a straight line above Kid's head.

4 Kid follows Rodrigo, rolling over his shoulder and landing mounted on Rodrigo. **Expert tip:** Make sure to roll over the shoulder, not straight over your head.

2 Sensing the counter, Kid changes his grips, moving them from Rodrigo's ankles to his wrists. Kid curls his legs back so that he can place his feet on Rodrigo's hips.

3 Kid extends his legs, pushing Rodrigo straight over his head.

The leg trap sweep from the closed guard is another great attack if your opponent stands up. In order for this sweep to work, the opponent's leg base can't be too wide. Although you might think that it's rare to stand with a narrow base, it can be a useful stance. Many times the passer will narrow his base so he can step back and press his forward knee between the defender's legs to break them open. You should initiate the sweep before your opponent steps back and just as he narrows his base.

1 Kid stands up while inside Rodrigo's closed guard.

2 Preparing to drive his right knee between Rodrigo's legs, Kid narrows his base by stepping his left foot in as he gets ready to step back with his left leg.

3 Before he can step back, Rodrigo opens his legs, drops his hips down towards the mat, and closes his legs around Kid's knees.

3 Detail correct Rodrigo locks his legs around Kid's knees.

3 Detail incorrect If he locks his legs below the knees, Kid can simply open up his knees and drop forward to the mat, which would open Rodrigo's legs and put Kid in a great guard passing position.

4 With his legs clamped together, Kid's base is destroyed. Rodrigo pulls Kid's left arm across his body and pressures his hips to the right, forcing Kid to fall.

5 Rodrigo continues to keep his legs locked around Kid's knees. As Kid falls to the side, Rodrigo pulls on the arm, using the momentum of the fall to pull himself up and over Kid. Rodrigo ends up mounted on Kid.

The windmill is another basic sweep from the guard that, based on your opponent's reaction, can work well in an attack combination. Again, the key is to sweep with the full intention of reversing your opponent, switching to another option only if your opponent properly counters it.

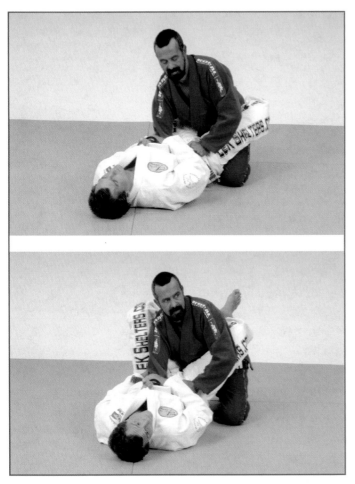

1 Rodrigo has Kid in the closed guard. Rodrigo controls Kid's right arm with both of his hands. He places his left foot on Kid's right hip, pushing off with it and sliding his hips slightly to the left, as if he were planning to attack Kid's right arm or sweep him to the right. In reaction, Kid raises his hips up.

2 Rodrigo turns his torso to the right and reaches his right hand around and behind Kid's left knee. At this point Rodrigo is ready to sweep Kid. He waits for Kid's slightest movement to initiate the windmill.

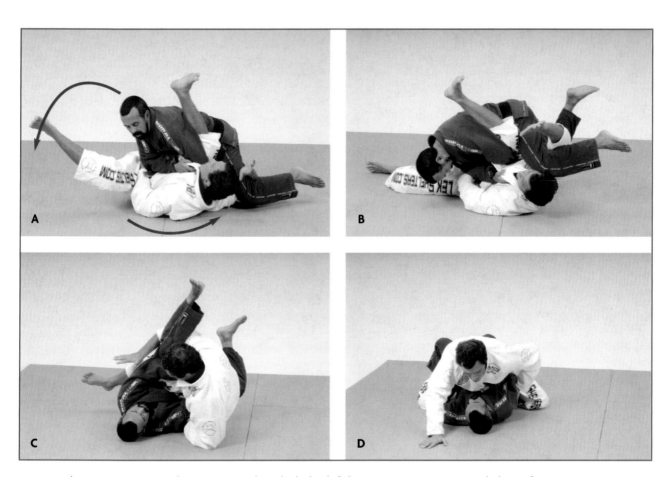

3 As Kid attempts to regain his posture Rodrigo kicks his left leg out, creating a counter balance for momentum. He kicks his right leg forward and toward his own left shoulder, hooking it under Kid's left arm and driving his torso to the left at the same time. Along with this movement, Rodrigo pulls up with his right arm, forcing Kid's left leg up and adding to the sweep over Kid's right shoulder. Since Kid's right hand is blocked by Rodrigo's left hand, he can't block the sweep. Rodrigo ends up mounted on Kid. **Expert tip:** During the sweep, never let go of your opponent's arm! The kicking motion of Rodrigo's leg is up and to the left. To get in the best angle to kick, Rodrigo needs to use his right arm to pull his torso towards Kid's left knee. Also, Kid is swept *over his shoulder,* not off to the side!

When applying the windmill, your opponent can raise his body and plant his leg out, gaining balance and blocking the sweep. This is one of the most common defenses against the windmill. But, as he reacts, he makes himself vulnerable to an arm-lock. Here's the key: Don't release your grip on the arm that you're sweeping over.

1 Rodrigo has initiated his windmill sweep to Kid's right side; he controls Kid's right arm and, has lassoed Kid's left leg with his right arm. As Rodrigo begins the windmill motion, kicking the left leg out for momentum, Kid raises his hips and leans back.

2 Kid opens his right leg out, plants the foot on the mat to block the sweep, and extends his body for posture. Realizing that his sweep is blocked, Rodrigo doesn't let go of Kid's right arm. Instead, he circles and locks his left leg back and over Kid's head, extending his body and driving his hips against Kid's right elbow to complete the arm-lock.

Many times, when faced with the windmill sweep, the opponent will try to counter it by leaning his weight to the opposite side of the attack. In this case, Rodrigo takes advantage of the lean and rolls to the same side that Kid leans, sweeping him.

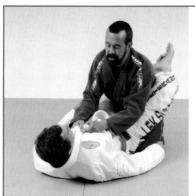

1 Rodrigo has Kid in the closed guard. He prepares the windmill sweep to Kid's right; with his left hand he holds Kid's right arm, with his right, he holds Kid's pants near the left ankle. Threatened by the sweep, Kid leans to his left – the opposite side of the attack – and plants his left arm on the mat. Rodrigo opens his legs, plants the left foot on Kid's right hip and pushes off with it, turning his body to the right.

2 Rodrigo continues to turn to the right as he grabs Kid's left arm with his right hand, pulling it off the mat and breaking the brace. Since Kid was leaning towards the brace, he can't help but fall to that side.

3 Rodrigo continues turning to the right. When his chest is flat on the mat, he opens his right arm and pushes off it, completing the roll and ending up mounted on Kid. Notice, throughout the entire movement, Rodrigo never releases Kid's left arm.

This variation is used when the opponent places his bracing arm out wide. He can place his arm out wide in the very beginning, or move the arm in and out, attempting to protect it from your grip as a defense against the previous move.

1 Rodrigo initiates the windmill sweep towards Kid's right, but Kid counters by leaning hard to the left and planting his left arm out wide as a brace keeping it away from Rodrigo's reach. Rodrigo has his left foot on Kid's right hip and his right hand gripping Kid's pants near the left ankle.

2 Rodrigo realizes that he can't initiate the roll over; Kid has too much weight on his bracing arm. Instead, he releases his right hand grip on Kid's pants and grabs Kid's left wrist. Rodrigo coils his right leg in and places the foot against Kid's left biceps, pushing off as if to pull Kid's left hand in for the roll over. Kid reacts to this by driving his body against the push. Rodrigo moves the right foot off Kid's biceps and as Kid falls forward, shoots it up to the left while moving his hips to the left. He locks the leg behind Kid's neck.

3 Rodrigo grabs his right ankle with his left hand, pulling it towards himself and securing the lock around Kid's right arm and head. Rodrigo then hooks his left leg over his right foot, locking the figure four, around Kid's head and arm to finish the triangle. **Expert tip:** To make sure Kid doesn't counter the triangle, Rodrigo holds Kid's left arm open. If he didn't, Kid could grab Rodrigo's collar and stack his legs over his head.

If your opponent tries to counter the windmill sweep by leaning and bracing, the key-lock is a great attack option. It's an extremely effective and surprising move that will give you a lot of submissions. Notice that this submission variation can be used from various positions, both in the closed and open guard, so be alert for the opportunity to use it when the arm is semi-extended and the elbow is crossed in front of your chest.

1 Rodrigo has initiated his windmill, but Kid counters by leaning to his left, opening his left arm and bracing with it. Rodrigo grabs Kid's right elbow with his left hand and Kid's pants at the left ankle with the right hand. Rodrigo begins to turn his body to the right, but Kid's solid brace stops him. Rodrigo then moves his torso to the left in a clockwise direction, while, at the same time, using his left hand to push and bend Kid's right elbow down. Rodrigo presses down against Kid's right shoulder with his left thigh, preventing Kid from escaping the arm.

2 Rodrigo loops his left leg over Kid's right shoulder, locking the left foot under the right, trapping Kid's shoulder. Rodrigo turns his torso further left, forcing Kid's body down. With both hands, Rodrigo grabs Kid's right hand; his left grips the top of Kid's hand, his right grips Kid's wrist and forces it up towards his own shoulder. Notice that Kid's elbow is blocked by Rodrigo's right thigh and Rodrigo drives his left leg down on Kid's right shoulder locking it in place, so as Rodrigo rotates Kid's wrist up it torques the shoulder joint for the key-lock submission

2 Detail Notice how Rodrigo grabs the top of Kid's hands—his fingers wrap over Kid's fingers and touch the palm. With this grip, Rodrigo not only gains leverage, but can also apply a wrist-lock. Also, Rodrigo's left hand firmly grips Kid's wrist.

At times, when trying to counter the windmill by bracing and leaning the opposite way, the opponent will be too focused on avoiding the sweep and, forgetting about his grip on the collar, will overextend it. In this situation, the arm-lock is the best and quickest solution.

1 Kid defends against the windmill sweep by leaning to his left, bracing on his left arm. Rodrigo tries to roll over to Kid's left, but this leads to a slight stalemate. Rodrigo turns his torso to the left and turns his torso to the left extending Kid's right arm.

2 In one quick motion Rodrigo pushes off his right leg against Kid's left side, switches his right hand grip from Kid's right leg to the right wrist and, at the same time, slides his left knee in front of Kid's neck until he can hook his foot behind, and press his shin against, it. Rodrigo continues turning to his left driving his hips against Kid's right elbow and completing the arm-lock.

OPEN GUARD TECHNIQUES

Once your guard is open and you can't easily close it again, you have entered the open guard territory. The open guard is extremely effective for sweeps and submissions and many of the same sequences presented in the closed guard section will work here with minor modifications.

Unlike the closed guard, the open guard has many variations. The most common ones are: the traditional open guard (one foot on the hip and one foot on the biceps), the butterfly or sitting guard (hooks inside and under the opponent's thighs), and the spider guard (both feet pushing against the opponent's biceps while the hands control both wrists). Other, more advanced techniques, such as the De La Riva guard (one leg wrapped around the opponent's leg while the other presses against the biceps), the X-guard (both legs wrapped under the opponent's legs in the shape of an X), are too specialized for the spectrum of this book. Here, we will concentrate on the essential ones; the traditional, butterfly and spider guard.

Traditional Open Guard

The traditional open guard – one foot on the hip and one foot on the biceps (and some other variations) – is an extremely versatile and effective guard, both for attacks and sweeps. It works equally well, with some minor variations, in Gi, No-Gi and No Holds Barred. This position is effective because, while you can fight with all four limbs, your opponent can only use his arms. Of course, there are ways for the passer to incorporate his legs, but most of the time, he needs them to maintain his base. Generally, in the traditional open guard, your opponent will only have his arms to break your defensive barrier.

Grips:
Generally, the defender has one hand controlling the passer's sleeve and one hand controlling his ankle or pant legs:
The sleeve control is similar to the spider guard (see figure 1)
The ankle control can be:
- Gripping the pants (see figure 2)
- Gripping the back of the ankle (see figure 3)
- Cannot be gripping the inside of the pants (illegal) (see figure 4)

figure 1

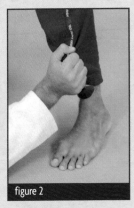
figure 2

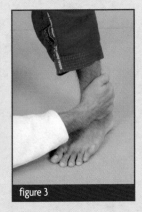
figure 3

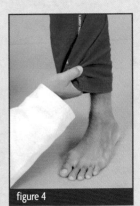
figure 4

Do's:
- Apply leg pressure on the hip and the arm that you don't control the grip (see figure 5)
- Shift your leg pressure from one leg to the other
- Remain connected with your opponent

Don'ts:
- Don't allow your opponent to control both legs (see figure 6)
- Don't let your opponent walk back and away from you
- Don't let him pin your legs down to the mat (see figure 7)
- Don't let him get too close to you crushing your legs
- Don't let him lift your legs and deflect their power upwards

figure 5

figure 6

figure 7

One of the greatest advantages to the open guard is the ability to quickly get the opponent off balance by using your legs and arms to push and pull him. The smart guard fighter takes advantage of the opponent's reaction to the push or the pull and applies the proper technique according to where the opponent's body weight is going. In other words, generally the person reacts to a push by pushing back. At that moment you would use a sweep that takes advantage of the opponent's weight commitment pushing back. In this case the perfect set up for the tripod sweep is for you to have pulled your opponent to you and he is fighting to get away.

1 Kid has Rodrigo in the open guard; his right foot pressed against Rodrigo's left biceps, his left foot pressing against Rodrigo's right hip, his right hand controlling Rodrigo's right arm and his left hand grabbing the back of Rodrigo's right ankle. To set up the move, Kid pulls Rodrigo's arm and ankle towards himself and waits for Rodrigo to fight and try to escape.

2 When Rodrigo reacts by leaning back, Kid moves his right leg and hooks the foot behind Rodrigo's left knee. He then extends his left leg, pushing Rodrigo's hips back while at the same time, pulls his right leg in forcing Rodrigo's left leg to buckle. Kid's left hand prevents Rodrigo's right leg from stepping back, causing him to lose his balance and fall backwards.

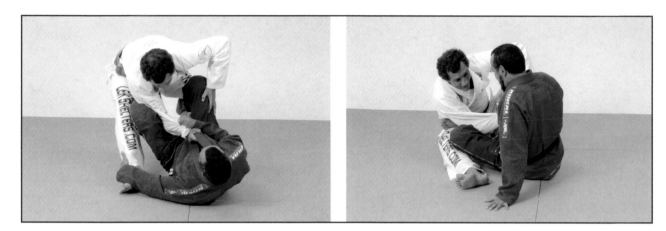

3 As Rodrigo falls back, the weight comes off his right leg and Kid pulls the foot up, making the fall much harder. Kid continues to hold Rodrigo's right sleeve with his right hand and pulls himself up, aided by Rodrigo's falling momentum. At the moment when both Kid and Rodrigo have their buttocks on the mat, there could be a stalemate. To break it and win the position by coming over the top, Kid posts his left hand back and pushes off with it. **Expert tip:** If Rodrigo manages to regain his balance and attempts to get up, Kid would simply pull Rodrigo's left ankle up with his left hand, preventing Rodrigo from getting back up.

4 Because Kid holds Rodrigo's right arm with his right arm, Rodrigo can't post his arm back and fight the mount of Rodrigo's right side. If Kid tries to climb to Rodrigo's left side, Rodrigo could post his left arm and fight the position. Kid moves his right foot back and plants it on the mat, while sliding his left foot down and hooking it under Rodrigo's right thigh. Kid pushes off with his right foot as he climbs to the top; to help in the movement, he pivots off his left arm and, pulls Rodrigo's right arm with his right hand. **Expert tip:** Notice that Kid doesn't let his body come straight up and over Rodrigo. Instead, he drops the left knee to the mat, shifts his weight and leans to the left, climbing with his hips towards the left. Kid ends up mounted on Rodrigo.

In the most common counter to the push pull sweep, your opponent would buckle in his right knee and twist his hips, deflecting your foot push. When this happens, you need to take advantage of your opponent's reaction, rather than fight for the sweep, and switch to the tripod sickle sweep.

1 Kid attempts the tripod push-pull sweep, but Rodrigo counters it by turning in his knee and twisting the hips to the left, deflecting the power of Kid's push.

2 Kid immediately switches to the sickle sweep by changing the control grip on Rodrigo's right sleeve; he moves his left hand from Rodrigo's right leg to the right sleeve. Kid shifts his hips to the left as he grabs the back of Rodrigo's left ankle with his right hand.

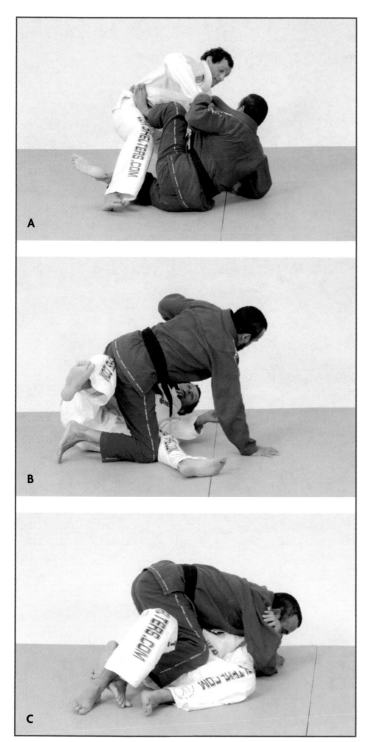

3 Once he has proper control, Kid drops his right leg to the ground and circles it counterclockwise, moving Rodrigo's right foot out to the right and collapsing his base. As the same time, Kid pushes off with his left foot, driving Rodrigo's hips, and causing him to fall, backwards. Kid's right hand prevents Rodrigo from stepping back with his left foot and regaining his base. Kid uses Rodrigo's weight momentum to help pull himself up by holding on to Rodrigo's right sleeve with his left hand. Kid plants the right arm on the mat to help get on top of Rodrigo completing the sweep.

In addition to sweeps, the open guard is also great for submissions. All submission sequences in the closed guard are also found in the open guard. In the next few techniques, we'll demonstrate a few of these sequences, but don't let this limit you—you can mix the sequences just as in the closed guard, and even create your own variations. Also, with just a little modification, these same techniques will also work in the spider guard.

With your opponent's arms extended and your legs already up, you can quickly attack with many staple jiu-jitsu submissions. The triangle is readily available whenever your opponent allows you to pull on of his arms down while pushing the other one up.

1 Rodrigo has Kid in the open guard. His right leg pushes against Kid's left biceps, while his right hand controls Kid's left sleeve. His left foot presses against Kid's right hip and his left hand controls Kid's right sleeve. Kid allows Rodrigo to pull his arm a little too far—setting him up for the triangle.

2 All in one motion: Rodrigo pushes off with his left foot, raises his hips, releases his right foot's pressure on Kid's left biceps and pulls Kid's right arm with his left, which causes Kid's torso to fall forward. Rodrigo immediately shoots the right leg straight up, raising his hips until his knee is past Kid's head. **Expert tip:** It's extremely important to have your hips close to the joint (in this case the neck) that you're attacking.

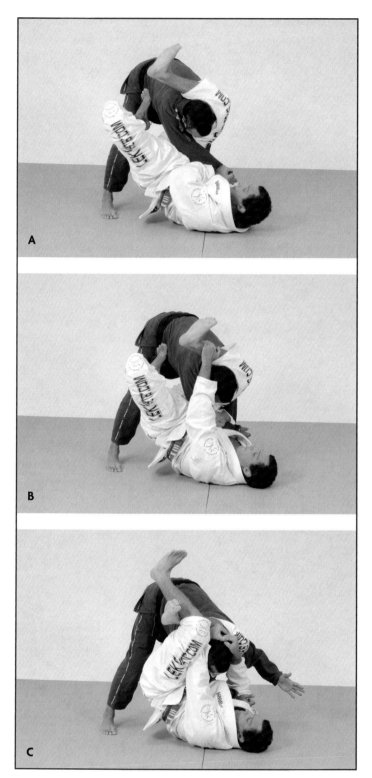

A

B

C

3 Rodrigo turns his torso to the right as he pulls Kid's right arm across his body with his left hand. Rodrigo drives his right heel down, forcing the calf down on Kid's neck, and moves his right hand grip to Kid's right elbow. Rodrigo grabs his right ankle with his left hand, loops the left leg over the right foot and locks, in a figure four, around Kid's right arm and head for the triangle choke. Rodrigo applies the choking pressure by squeezing his knees together and pulling down on Kid's head with his hands.

Having your opponent worry about your open guard attacks is a great advantage in a match. When you have him worrying about the submissions it will open up the sweeps and vice-versa. As we said before, the triangle, the arm-lock and the omoplata work well in conjunction. In this case, Rodrigo attacks with the triangle and Kid responds by posturing up, straightening his spine and putting his head up. This is the perfect moment for Rodrigo to switch to the arm-lock.

1 Rodrigo has Kid in the open guard. Rodrigo pulls Kid's left arm down as he shoots his right leg up. He lifts his hips and simultaneously initiates the triangle (similar to technique 85).

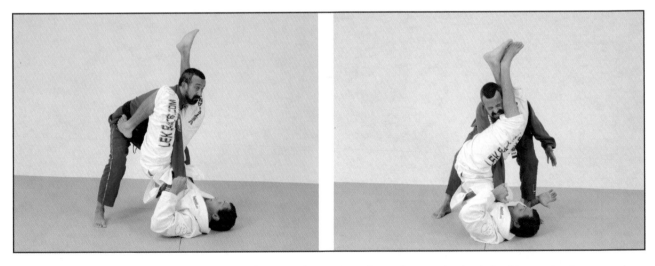

2 Sensing the triangle attack, Kid counters it by raising his torso and straightening his back. Rodrigo maintains control over Kid's right arm with his left arm and quickly switches to the arm-lock. He loops his right arm inside of Kid's left leg and uses it to help pull his hips up, turn his body to the right and loop the left leg over Kid's head. Rodrigo stretches his body, driving his hips against Kid's elbow hyperextending it for the arm-lock.

Many times opponents are so leery of the triangle-arm-lock combination that it is hard to surprise them with those attacks. A great option that works well in conjunction with this combination, as we've mentioned before, is the omoplata (shoulder-lock). Here Rodrigo demonstrates one of the best set-ups for the omoplata from the open guard. **Expert tip:** Rodrigo sets up the move much like he would set up the triangle or the arm-lock except he turns the hips slightly towards the arm that he wants to attack giving him a triple option from the same set-up.

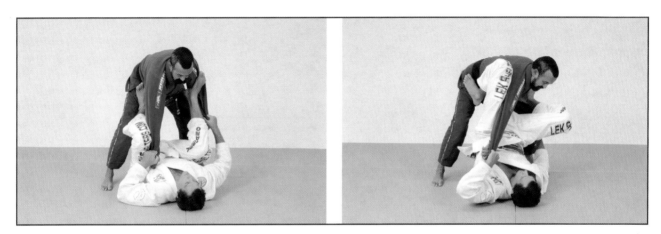

1 Rodrigo has Kid in the open guard: his right foot pressing against Kid's left biceps, his left foot pushing against Kid's right hip. Rodrigo controls Kid's sleeves with his hands. Rodrigo pushes off his feet raising his hips while turning them to the right so they are touching Kid's right arm. **Expert tip:** As we have pointed out several times in order to be the most effective and leave the least amount of space for the opponent to escape, your hips should be near the joint that you want to attack (in this example, Rodrigo's hips are raised towards Kid's right shoulder).

2 Rodrigo shoots the left leg up wrapping it around Kid's right arm as he turns his torso to the left. The pressure of Rodrigo's leg on Kid's arm forces him down to the mat. Rodrigo plants his right foot on the mat and uses it to continue turning his torso to the left as he grabs Kid's belt with his left hand – the elbow down and tight against the back – securing the omoplata. All Rodrigo needs to do to get the submission is to sit up to apply the pressure.

Spider Guard

This is a variation of the traditional open guard. While in the traditional open guard you grip one sleeve and have one foot on the hip and one foot on the biceps. In the spider guard you grip both of your opponent's sleeves while placing your feet against his biceps. Once you establish this position, push up with your feet and pull his hands down. This gives you complete control of his arms, as if they were puppets.

Because you need to control the sleeves, the spider guard isn't very effective for mixed martial arts or submission grappling although it's possible to adapt the spider guard for these situations. But because it's such a great platform for sweeps, the spider guard is a favorite for sports Jiu-Jitsu, especially for those interested in competing in tournaments.

Do's (see figure 1):
Rodrigo uses the spider guard against Kid.
- Shift pressure from one leg to another so that your opponent is never completely settled or comfortable.
- Keep your elbows bent and close to your body
- Make sure that your foot pressure keeps your opponent's elbows bent
- If you want to sweep him, you'll need to stay close
- Keep steady pressure

figure 1

Don'ts (see figure 2):
Kid improperly applies the spider guard against Rodrigo.
- Extend your arms
- Allow your opponent to come too close or control your pant legs
- Apply extreme pressure, which will waste energy
- Allow your opponent to move away from you

figure 2

Spider guard control options

Sleeve grip:

Foot placement:

Incorrect By grabbing the inside of the cloth, you won't gain the necessary control.

Correct Grab your opponent's cuff with your hand curling the cloth from the outside in.

Incorrect If you place the heel on his biceps, it will most likely slip over the top.

Correct Place the ball of your foot on your opponent's biceps and push against it so that his elbow is bent.

Foot Placement Options:

Traditional placement: each foot presses against the biceps on the same side of the body. Advantages: good for control, sweeps and attacks. Disadvantages: Easier for your opponent to move away, easier to break the pressure and control.

One foot on the biceps and the other hooked inside the leg on the same side. Advantages: Good for sweeps, good for stopping your opponent from moving away. Disadvantages: Not as good for triangles and arm-locks.

One foot looped around the arm and the other hooking the leg. Advantage: great control over the opponent, good for sweeps. Disadvantages: Exposes the foot and knee to submissions, higher chance of catching your foot in the gi and hurting your foot while twisting.

A very common occurrence when using the spider guard is for the opponent to control both your legs and push them to the mat, pinning your legs with his weight. Of course, the best option is to avoid his grip or, if he gets it, immediately break it as shown in the introductory section. Unfortunately, you won't always be able to react in time. This technique can effectively remedy the problem.

1 Kid has Stefano in the spider guard. Stefano is able to control both ankles, extend his arms to release the pressure, walk back, push the ankles to the mat and pin them down. Once Kid realizes that he's lost control of his legs, he immediately sits up, otherwise Stefano can easily walk around his side and pass his guard.

2 Kid braces his left arm back and grabs the back of Stefano's right arm at or above the elbow with his right hand. In one move; Kid pushes off his left arm, escaping the hips hard to the left, and pulls Stefano's right arm forward with his right hand. Since Stefano had his weight forward and on his hands, he falls forward to the mat as Kid moves away and pulls out the arm.

3 Kid wraps his arms around Stefano's hips and moves to Stefano's back.

Another option for the same situation is presented here, as it is quite common for the passer to have his head down as he goes for this type of pass (toreana or "bull fighter's" pass). In this case perhaps Stefano has his head down and is not as committed with his weight forward, or perhaps Kid simply wants the submission, so he goes for the loop choke. We pick up the technique from the moment that Stefano has broken the spider guard and pins Kids legs to the mat. Note: If Stefano has his head up, this technique will not work.

1 Stefano pins Kid's legs to the mat. Kid sits up, braces with his left arm posted behind him and grabs Stefano's right collar with his right hand. Kid wants to use the loop choke, since he has his right hand on Stefano's collar, he needs to bait Stefano to pass towards the left. To do this, he drops his left knee on the mat, giving Stefano a clear path to that side. If Stefano decides to pass towards the right, Kid can simply raise his right elbow, force his forearm against Stefano's throat and push off with his left arm, moving his hips to the right blocking Stefano's path. **Expert tip:** Don't grab your opponent's collar too tightly against his neck, otherwise you'll reveal your real intentions.

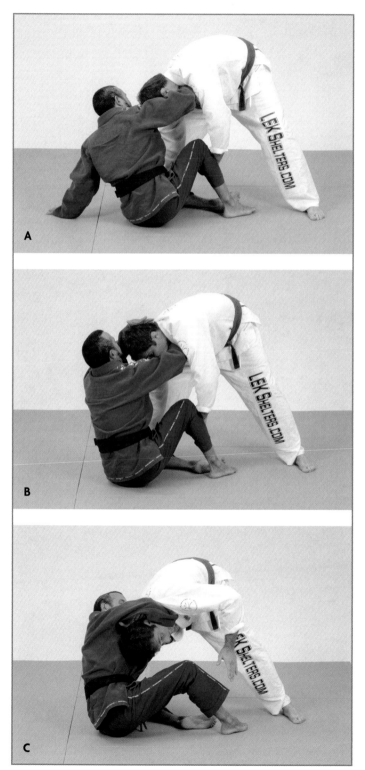

A

B

C

2 Seeing a clear path, Stefano approaches Kid's left, stepping with his right foot. Kid allows Stefano to come forward. Then, in a sudden movement, Kid quickly sits further up, pushes down on the back of Stefano's head with his left hand and loops his right elbow over it. The choke is set: Stefano's collar pulled by Kid's right arm looped around Stefano's neck. Kid leans to the left, slides his left arm over Stefano's head and loops his hand inside his right arm, tightening the collar around Stefano's neck and adding pressure to the choke.

Sometimes, you might not be quick enough, allowing your opponent to pin your legs and actually start to pass. In order to pass, your opponent will most likely kneel, or step around your legs or body, and put weight on you by dropping his head and shoulder on your chest. If this happens, you can use this technique to defend the pass.

1 Rodrigo is able to control Kid's legs and pin them to the ground. He kneels down next to Kid's legs and puts his weight on them, controlling them as he walks to Kid's right side.

2 Kid sits up, plants both hands on the mat and scoots his hips to the left (away from Rodrigo's direction of pass).

3 Kid puts his left hand on the right side of Rodrigo's face and forces it down to the mat. Kid continues to push off with his left hand and moves his hips further to the left. As he moves away, Kid redirects Rodrigo's pressure to the side, reducing Rodrigo's control and allowing Kid to pull his legs away.

Incorrect Kid pushes the left side of Rodrigo's face with his right hand. Notice that this is Rodrigo's natural direction of movement; he can pivot around Kid's hand and reach side control. Not only does Kid fail to reduce the pressure, but he also gives Rodrigo a good pivot point for the pass.

As pointed out before, many of the sweeps and attacks presented in the traditional open guard section will, with a few minor modifications, work in the spider guard. This sweep is the most basic of the spider guard sweeps, the key to this sweep is to maintain pressure on the leg of the side your are sweeping to (opposite to the side your opponent tries to pass) and then using it as a piston with a quick coil and extension redirecting the opponent's weight to accomplish the sweep.

1 Kid has Stefano in the open guard; his hands control Stefano's sleeves, his feet press against Stefano's biceps.

A   B   C

2 Stefano moves, attempting to pass the guard to Kid's right. In response, Kid, while pulling Stefano's right sleeve with his left hand, pushes with his left foot and coils his right leg in, blocking Stefano's hips with the shin. Kid grabs Stefano's left leg with his right hand. As long as Kid keeps his left leg pushing Stefano's right arm away, Stefano won't be able to gain side control. When Stefano tries to secure the pass by placing his weight on Kid, Kid uses his left leg as a piston to initiate the sweep, first giving in a little, then pushing out to the left. The pressure on Stefano's right arm forces his torso to lean over to the direction of the sweep; his body is extended and his weight and hips rest on Kid's right shin. Kid helps the sweep pulling Stefano's left leg with his right hand moving it over the top of his body in a circular motion. Notice, during the entire sweep, Kid's hands and legs move in a big circle.

A

B

C

3 As Stefano's body lands, Kid releases his left foot's pressure on Stefano's biceps. Kid continues to pull on Stefano's right sleeve with his left arm, and drive Stefano's left leg over with the right arm. Kid continues to climb on top of Stefano, bracing with both arms to maintain the position. He opens his left leg out and ends up with his right knee on Stefano's stomach. Notice, throughout the sweep, Kid right shin was in front of Stefano's hips, already positioned for the knee on the stomach.

At times when faced with the spider guard sweep your opponent might try to counter the sweep instead of continuing with his passing motion. He might be able to stop your sweep by stepping in, posturing his body up and, just as you switch your grips from his sleeves to his pants, putting his weight on top of you. When faced with this defense, you should respond with this variation of the sickle sweep.

1 As Kid changes his grip and prepares to initiate the traditional spider guard sweep, Stefano, sensing the oncoming attack, counters it by posturing and straightening his body rather than placing his weight on Kid.

2 Kid immediately changes to the sickle sweep. He moves his left foot from Stefano's right biceps to the stomach and uses his right hand to help pull his torso to the right. Kid kicks his right heel to the left bringing the leg across the mat in a circular motion hooking and removing Stefano's right foot brace. At the same time, Kid extends his left leg, pushing Stefano's hips back and forcing him to fall backwards.

3 As Stefano falls back, Kid uses the falling momentum to come up and over, propping himself up with his left hand's grip on Stefano's right sleeve. He ends on top, his right leg still hooked on Stefano's right leg.

4 Still pulling up on Stefano's right arm, Kid steps back with his left leg, raises his right knee, and circles it over the top of Stefano's right leg making sure his right foot hooks the leg. Kid hooks his right arm under Stefano's left arm and places his weight to his hips. Kid then releases the right foot hook, squares his body above Stefano and reaches side control.

If your opponent never stands up and tries to pass low, you can use the same traditional sweep. In that case you can either use the extended leg or the coiled one as Rodrigo demonstrates here.

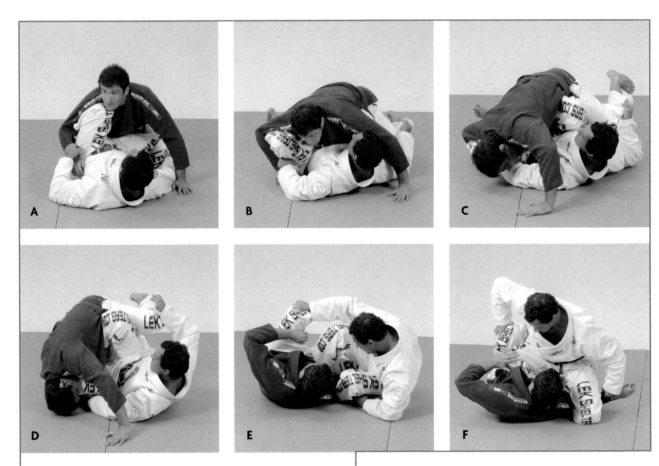

1 If your opponent doesn't stand up, the motion is exactly the same as in the spider guard sweep (shown in technique 92). **Expert tip:** Since the motion has less amplitude than the stand-up sweep, you'll have to exert greater pressure against his hips with your shin. This will keep him away and prevent him from pushing the hips down and locking his body on yours.

When executing a low spider guard sweep, your opponent will sometimes grab around your neck with his arm. While this can make the sweep more difficult, it also exposes his arm to an arm-lock.

1 Rodrigo sets up the low spider guard sweep, but Stefano counters by reaching with his left arm and grabbing the back of Rodrigo's neck.

2 Rodrigo immediately releases his handgrips on Stefano's left leg and right sleeve, wrapping them around Stefano's left elbow as he extends and turns his body to the left. **Expert tip:** Rodrigo traps Stefano's wrist by tilting his head to the right. He places his right arm with his elbow over Stefano's left elbow and holds his own gi with that hand. Rodrigo uses his left hand to pull his right elbow in adding greater pressure on Stefano's elbow.

An effective counter to the spider low pass sweep is for the opponent to lean to the opposite side of the sweep making it harder to execute the move. While this makes it harder to execute the sweep, it becomes easier for you to take his back.

1 Rodrigo attempts to use the low spider guard sweep, but Stefano counters the sweep by leaning to the left. At this point, there's a stalemate; Rodrigo pushing his left leg against Stefano's right arm, Stefano leaning right to counter the pressure.

2 Rodrigo quickly extends his left leg, shooting it forward and releasing the pressure on Stefano's right arm. Taking advantage of this release, Rodrigo uses his left arm to drive Stefano's right arm across his body exposing Stefano's back.

3 Rodrigo wraps his arms around Stefano's waist as he kneels behind him and takes his back.

When your opponent counters by leaning away, you may prefer this to taking the back. Both are good options; both are considered sweeps in Brazilian Jiu-Jitsu competition and both yield 2 points. In the previous technique, you place hooks and earn an additional 4 points. In this move, you can pass the guard and reach side control, earning 3 extra points.

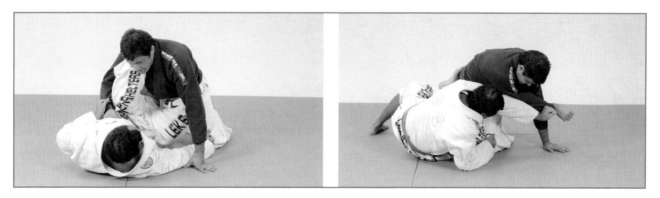

1 Rodrigo attempts the sweep, but Stefano leans away and counters it. Rodrigo quickly shoots his left leg out and pushes Stefano's right arm across his body with his left hand.

2 Rodrigo kneels down next to Stefano while still pushing the arm across. He grabs Stefano's left leg at the knee with his right hand and pulls it in while using his head and left shoulder to push Stefano's torso to the mat for the sweep.

3 Rodrigo continues to force Stefano's arm and leg down, pinning them to the mat, as he drives his body over and around Stef's hips ending up in side control completing the pass.

Butterfly Guard

The butterfly, or sitting guard, is a common and extremely useful position for sweeping your opponent. To properly position yourself, you should be sitting up with your hips back. Your head should be centered and pushing against your opponent's chest. Bend your legs, knees pointing out and feet hooked under your opponent's thighs. You should place your arms under your opponent's arms, with your hands either grabbing the belt or locked around his back (see photo below). Alternatively, your arms can be in front of the opponent's arms, the hands grabbing the elbows or one elbow and a shoulder.

Do's (see figure 1):
Kid properly applies the butterfly guard against Rodrigo.
- Sit up
- Keep your knees open
- Keep your hips away from your opponent until you initiate a sweep
- To control the distance, keep your head in the center and under your opponent's head
- Keep your feet curled in, acting like hooks

figure 1

figure 2

Don'ts:
Kid improperly applies the butterfly guard against Rodrigo.
- Allow your back to rest on the ground (see figure 2)
- Keep your knees together (see figure 3)
- Allow your opponent's head to be lower than yours, particularly on the chest, which would give him control of both distance and the center (see figure 4)
- Keep your hips too close to your opponent (see figure 5)
- Have your toes pointing forward, which will cause them to slip out when executing a sweep

figure 3

figure 4

figure 5

In the butterfly guard sweep, arguably the staple move of this guard, you use your foot, which is hooked under your opponent's leg, to lift and reverse him from top to bottom. There are several important keys for this sweep. The most important is that you don't sweep to the side or over your back. Rather, you need to sweep over, and roll towards, your shoulder. If you roll towards to the side the opponent can brace easily and if you go over your back, you will be flat on the mat, stopping your motion.

1 Kid has Rodrigo in the butterfly guard. His right hand is under Rodrigo's left arm and grips his belt, while his right foot is hooked under Rodrigo's left thigh. Kid grabs Rodrigo's right arm with his left hand, preventing him from opening it and bracing. Notice, since Kid is sweeping to the left, his hips moved slightly to the right.

2 Kid initiates the sweep as he pulls Rodrigo's belt with his right hand, forcing the torso to fall forward so his weight rests on Kid's leg. At the same time, Kid drops his head to the ground and towards his left shoulder to generate momentum, and kicks up with his right leg lifting Rodrigo's left leg up and over. Kid pulls Rodrigo's right arm in with his left hand rotating Rodrigo's torso in the same direction, eliminating any chance for Rodrigo to post the arm out, brace and stop the sweep. Kid tucks his left foot in; if he needs, he can push off with his toes to assist in the sweep. Notice, at this point, Kid could release his right foot hook, slide it under Rodrigo's left arm and take his back.

2 **Reverse view** Alternative grip. Rather than grab the opponent's belt, many fighters prefer to grab his pants at the knee. Both ways work. It's completely a matter of personal preference.

2 **Incorrect** Instead of rolling over the left shoulder, Kid rolls backwards. This is a common mistake for beginners. In this case, his back hits flat on the mat. This not only stops Kid's motion, but also puts Rodrigo's weight on top, rather than making it fall to the open side of the mat.

3 Rodrigo's torso is still twisting around as Kid's shoulder touches the mat. Kid continues lifting his right leg elevating Rodrigo's left leg to complete the sweep. Kid ends up mounted on Rodrigo. Notice, since the sweep was over the shoulder and not to the side, Kid doesn't finish perpendicular to Rodrigo, but leaning slightly forward.

3 Reverse Notice how Kid's right foot hooks under Rodrigo's left leg above the knee. Kid kicks the right leg up and fully extends it, lifting Rodrigo's left leg up and over.

Often, when executing the butterfly sweep, an opponent manages to open his knee widely out and block your sweep. When this happens, rather than fight with brute force for the sweep, simply use your other leg to remove his block.

1 Kid initiates a butterfly sweep to the left, but Rodrigo quickly opens out his right knee and braces against the sweep. Since Rodrigo's brace stops Kid's motion, there's a slight stalemate. Kid keeps pulling Rodrigo's belt up with his right hand; if he doesn't, Rodrigo can move back and make the sweep even more difficult.

2 Kid kicks his left leg open and places it in front of Rodrigo's right knee, moving it towards the right in a scissoring motion. **Expert tip:** Notice, as we pointed out in the "Do's and Don'ts" section, it's extremely important for Kid's hips to keep away from Rodrigo's hips. If he doesn't, Kid's left leg would be stuck inside Rodrigo's leg and couldn't slide in front of it.

A

B

C

3 Kid's scissoring motion removes Rodrigo's right knee block. Kid continues the sweep, dropping his head towards his left shoulder, kicking his right leg up ending up mounted on Rodrigo.

Countering the previous technique, your opponent might be able to open his leg even wider, achieving a better brace and successfully defending the sweep. As in the last technique, instead of wasting your energy with brute force, a slight adjustment will work much better. We pick up the position with Rodrigo opening out his right knee and stopping the initial sweep.

1 Kid initiates the butterfly sweep to the left, but Rodrigo quickly opens out his right knee and braces against the sweep. Kid continues to pull Rodrigo's belt up with the right hand, keeping Rodrigo's weight forward and over his right leg. At this point, there's a slight stalemate as they fight for the position.

2 In the stalemate Rodrigo opens his right leg out planting the foot on the mat, improving his brace and further complicating the sweep. Notice that Kid's right leg is lifting Rodrigo's hips, making it easier for Rodrigo to open out his leg. Also notice that Kid maintains control over Rodrigo's right arm, pulling it in with his left hand so that Rodrigo can't gain another bracing point.

3 Kid opens out his left leg, extending the foot until it's in front of Rodrigo's right knee. Kid cups the foot, the toes pointing down and pressing against Rodrigo's knee. Kid continues the sweep. He extends his left leg, pushing Rodrigo's right leg back and removing the brace. At the same time, he raises Rodrigo's torso by pulling his belt and, with his extended right leg, lifts Kid's leg over. Kid ends up mounted on Rodrigo.

When executing the butterfly guard sweep, you will often be presented with the opportunity to take your opponent's back. It can occur as you execute the sweep, or during one of the stalemates when your opponent resists the move. Whenever it occurs, it's important to be aware and immediately take advantage of it. By adding this to your repertoire, you develop a new dimension to your butterfly guard, much like the double and triple attacks presented before. By having a solid combination option that works well with the butterfly guard – like taking the back – your sweeps will improve as your opponent now has to worry about giving up the back.

1 Rodrigo has Kid in the butterfly guard and is setting up a sweep to the right. With his right arm, Rodrigo pulls and tucks away Kid's left arm, eliminating any possibility of bracing on that side. Rodrigo's left foot hooked under Kid's right leg will act as an elevator, helping to throw Kid's body around as Rodrigo turns his body to the right and sweeps over his right shoulder. At the height of the sweep, Kid either resists or, trying to counter the sweep, leans forward too much. Rodrigo takes advantage and goes to the back.

2 Rodrigo continues to drive Kid's body forward by pulling his belt up towards his head. Rodrigo opens his left elbow up and ducks his head under Kid's right arm. Not only is Kid pulled forward, but Rodrigo also slides his body back, ending up behind Kid's back. As he gets behind Kid, Rodrigo releases his left foot hook, dropping Kid flat on the mat. Notice however that Rodrigo's right foot remains between Kid's legs ending up hooked around Kid's right leg as the first hook for taking and controlling the back. Rodrigo pushes down on Kid's belt with his left hand, forcing Kid's hips to the mat and preventing him from getting back up.

2 **Side angle** Notice how Rodrigo pulls Kid's torso up, not only driving Kid's torso forward, but also helping himself drop down. Also, notice how Rodrigo moves his left hook. He releases the hook as he gets around to Kid's back and switches to his right foot, which is already positioned to hook Kid's right leg.

3 Rodrigo loops his left leg over Kid's back, hooking the left foot on Kid's left leg for the second hook, taking the back.

When you attempt to take your opponent's back, he might block you by grabbing around your back with his arms. Since his arm is extended, the arm-bar is a great response.

1 Rodrigo has his left foot hooked under Kid's right leg. He initiates the butterfly sweep to the right, dropping his head towards his right shoulder and extending his left leg. As the left leg lifts Kid's right leg, Rodrigo pulls in Kid's left arm. Kid defends the sweep and Rodrigo responds by raising his left arm and begins to move towards Kid's back. Kid grabs Rodrigo's back with his right hand, preventing him from moving down and around to the back. Rodrigo drops his hips back to the mat and slides them away from Kid creating enough space for his right leg to slide in front of Kid's legs. It also forces Kid to slightly extend his right arm.

2 Rodrigo opens out his right leg and pushes the foot against Kid's left thigh. As he pushes off, Rodrigo moves his hips backwards and away from Kid, forcing Kid to flatten his body. Rodrigo's torso leans back, further extending Kid's right arm. Rodrigo turns his head slightly to the left, trapping Kid's arm between it and Kid's left shoulder. Notice that Rodrigo's grips are the same as the original butterfly guard sweep grips; his right hand controls Kid's left sleeve and his left hand pulls up on Kid's belt.

3 Rodrigo moves his torso further away from Kid and turns his body to the right (around Kid's right arm), as he drops his left leg over Kid's back sandwiching Kid's torso between his two legs. Rodrigo releases both hand grips and wraps his left arm around Kid's right elbow; Rodrigo's elbow is on top of Kid's elbow and the hand touches his own right shoulder. He presses against his own left elbow with his right hand, applying the pressure on Kid's elbow for the arm-bar. Notice, when applying pressure on Kid's elbow, Rodrigo keeps his body slightly curved. If Rodrigo's body was fully extended, Kid's arm would be flat, the elbow pressing against Rodrigo's belly, and wouldn't be hyper-extended.

4 If Kid somehow escapes the lock by slipping his wrist out from between Rodrigo's head and shoulder, Rodrigo quickly changes to a key-lock by keeping the left arm wrapped around Kid's right arm and exchanging the left hand from his own elbow to Kid's wrist. As soon as Rodrigo catches Kid's wrist with his left hand he locks his own left hand on his right wrist for the key-lock and applies the pressure to the shoulder by driving Kid's wrist to the left. **Expert tip:** From this position, the series of attacks from the "windmill sweep and arm wrap submission techniques" will work with some minor modifications.

At times the opponent is so defensive and wants to avoid engaging so much that he won't let you get your arm around him and grab his belt. He will keep you at distance. His hands may be busy trying to push one or both of your legs pinning them to the mat to pass your guard. A very effective attack from the butterfly guard when the opponent stays away is to use this combination: taking the back – sweep. In this combination, depending on your opponent's reaction, you can either take his back or sweep him.

1 Kid has Rodrigo in the butterfly guard; his feet hooked under Rodrigo's thighs. Rodrigo, however, has managed to stop Kid from engaging him, keeping his distance and blocking Kid from underhooking his arm and gripping the belt. Rodrigo wants to pin the legs to the mat in his attempt to pass. Kid has his right hand grabbing Rodrigo's right collar and his left hand controls Rodrigo's right hand at the wrist

2 Kid quickly grabs Rodrigo's right triceps with his right hand, pulling the arm forward and plants his left hand on the mat at the same time. Pushing off with his left hand, he scoots his hips to the left, driving Rodrigo's arm across Rodrigo's torso. **Expert tip:** Kid pulls Rodrigo's triceps right near the elbow, opening it up and applying a lot of pressure on the shoulder. This forces Rodrigo to release the grip on the pants and follow the pull. Kid ends up on Rodrigo's right side with his left arm grabbing Rodrigo's belt, the right arm hooked around Rodrigo's right arm and his foot hooks still in place and active. Also, if Rodrigo's elbow is tight against his torso it would be difficult for Kid to reach in for the arm drag. Kid would force the arm open by releasing the left foot hook from Rodrigo's right thigh and kicking the leg open carrying Rodrigo's right arm (hand grabbing the pants) out open with it so he can grab the arm.

3 If Rodrigo doesn't react Kid will simply release his left foot hook, loop the leg around Rodrigo's back and hook the left foot on Rodrigo's left hip – taking his back. Rodrigo doesn't want that so he counters by opening his left leg out posting the foot as far out as possible as he tries to raise his hips and pulls the right arm back across Kid's body. Rodrigo's reaction calls for an alternative, so Kid changes to the sweep. Kid changes the right hand from under Rodrigo's arm to the sleeve at the wrist and drops his right leg to ground. Kid pushes off the right foot to initiate the sweep as he leans back pulling Rodrigo's belt with his left hand. Kid kicks the left leg up, lifting Rodrigo's hips with the left foot pushing up on Rodrigo's right thigh. Kid rotates his body to the left, sweeping Rodrigo over. When Kid's back gets flat on the ground he needs to change hooks and uses the right foot to hook under Rodrigo's left leg kicking up and over completing the sweep. Kid ends up mounted on Rodrigo.

This is another great way to handle a defensive opponent who doesn't want to engage with you. You can use this alternative grip when using the butterfly guard. In this move, the key is to pull one of your opponent's elbows out and push the other in, as if you were turning a big steering wheel. Many people prefer this grip variation; the set up is much easier than sliding your arm under your opponent's arm. In this technique, you just need to grab, turn and presto—your opponent goes flying!

1 Rodrigo has Kid in the butterfly guard. Rodrigo has attempted to underhook one of Kid's arms and grab the belt, but Kid has managed to avoid it. Kid is staying away from Rodrigo and is busy using his hands trying to pin Rodrigo's legs to the mat for the pass. Rodrigo has each of his hands grabbing Kid's arms at the outside of the elbows

2 Rodrigo pushes Kid's left elbow in with his right hand as he pulls out Kid's right elbow with his left hand; just like he were turning a big wheel. At the same time Rodrigo uses his arms pushing and turning Rodrigo's arms to help scoot his hips in close to Kid. Rodrigo drops his right leg to the mat and keeps his left knee up so that he can hook the left foot under Kid's right thigh.

3 As Rodrigo continues to pull and push Kid's elbows, he drops his head to the right and rolls over his right shoulder while he kicks his left leg up, using his left foot hook to lift and help turn Kid's body around. Rodrigo ends with his knee on Kid's stomach in this case but could have just as easily ended up mounted by looping the left foot around Kid's right thigh as they rolled over.

NOTES